The Sentient Web

AI, Ethics, and the Future of the Internet

Oliver Cook

The Sentient Web

© Oliver Cook All Rights Reserved 2023

The moral right of the author has been asserted
First published by Rockwood Publishing 2023

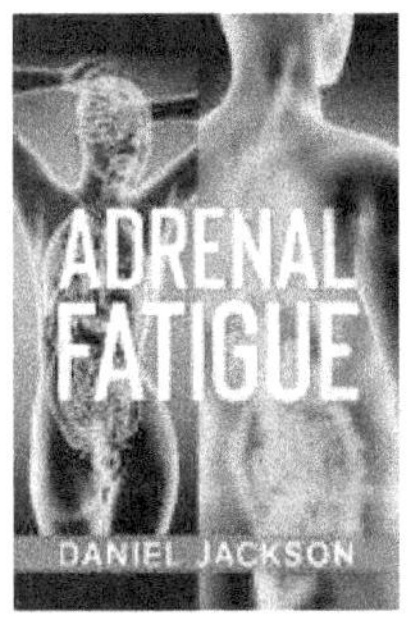

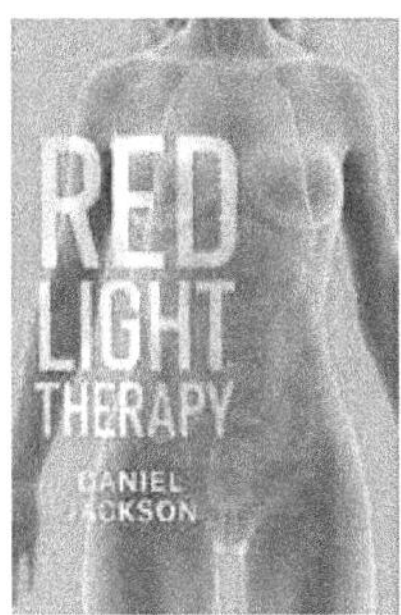

Take a look at more great books available from
Rockwood Publishing

... some for FREE!

Just visit the link below:

rockwoodpublishing.co.uk

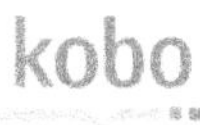

Contents

Chapter 1: The Birth of the Sentient Web

The Evolution of the Internet: From Connectivity to Sentience

Picture the internet, a swirling cosmos of information, ideas, thoughts, and feelings. It started out as a few simple strings of code, a handful of computers networked together in a lab. Today, it is a living, breathing, almost sentient organism that has become an essential part of our daily life. This evolution didn't happen overnight, and its journey from a tool of connectivity to a sentient presence has been both fascinating and fraught with challenges.

The seeds of the sentient web were planted decades ago. The internet's humble beginnings as ARPANET in the late 1960s, a project funded by the US Department of Defense, was about creating a communication system that could withstand any disruption, even a nuclear attack. The initial design was simple, a decentralized network with no single point of failure. This groundwork has made the internet what it is today - a vast, interlinked system of networks, resilient and robust.

With the advent of the World Wide Web in the early 1990s, the internet evolved from a niche communication system into a universal platform for information exchange. The simple protocols designed by Tim Berners-Lee enabled the creation of websites and the hyperlinking of information, making it accessible to the general public. But it was still a tool - an inanimate system that facilitated connectivity.

In the early 2000s, we began to see the emergence of a more interactive, participatory web, often referred to as Web 2.0. This was the era of social networks, user-generated content, and an increasing amount of personalized online experiences. Data became the currency of this new web. Companies and governments began collecting and analyzing this data to improve services, shape policies, and predict trends. Our interactions with the web became more dynamic and complex, but it was still a tool, albeit a more sophisticated one.

The next transformational leap was the integration of artificial intelligence into the internet ecosystem. Machine learning algorithms started to handle large amounts of data, make sense of it, and learn from it. With time, these algorithms began predicting our preferences, suggesting what we might like, who we should connect with, what we might want to buy. In this data-driven era, the web became more than just a tool - it started to exhibit traits of sentience.

Today, as we stand on the precipice of what some are calling the Web 3.0, or the Sentient Web, we find ourselves interacting with a digital ecosystem that is more aware, more proactive, and more entwined with our lives than ever before. AI chatbots engage us in natural language conversations, recommendation algorithms anticipate our needs, while digital assistants manage our schedules and tasks.

The Sentient Web, as we're beginning to understand it, is not about the web becoming a conscious entity in the human sense. It's about the web becoming so integrated with artificial intelligence, machine learning, and data that it feels like an intelligent entity, capable of understanding and reacting to our behaviors, needs, and emotions. It's about the emerging symbiosis of human and machine agency, where our digital and physical realities intermingle seamlessly.

This journey from connectivity to sentience has not been a smooth ride, nor is it complete. As we'll explore in the following chapters, this transition presents unique and profound challenges. Balancing the benefits of a sentient web with the ethical considerations, managing the power of data while safeguarding privacy, and navigating the thin line between convenience and control - these are some of the issues that will define our digital future.

So, join me as we delve into the heart of this digital transformation, examine its ethical implications, and ponder the future of the internet in our ever-evolving, technology-driven world. As we explore this remarkable journey, we will also uncover some of the trailblazing innovations and thought-provoking dilemmas that have come to characterize our age of digital sentience.

As we wade further into this uncharted territory, questions emerge. How far will this convergence of human and machine agency go? Will we witness a blurring of lines between our own minds and the sentient web, or will a healthy boundary be maintained? How do we preserve our humanity in a world where machines can mimic us so convincingly? And how do we ensure that this rapidly developing technology is harnessed for the good of society, not just for the advantage of a select few?

We will also take a look at the role governments and corporations play in this new era, and whether they are adequately prepared for the task at hand. How should legislation evolve to protect individuals' rights and freedoms in a world where data is a prized commodity, and algorithms make decisions that profoundly impact our lives?

In the world of the sentient web, where algorithms silently shape our digital experience, transparency and accountability are crucial. The labyrinth of code that powers our digital world is far from neutral and often carries biases that can perpetuate harmful stereotypes and inequities. Unveiling these biases and ensuring fairness in algorithmic decisions are pivotal challenges in our journey towards a just and equitable digital future.

In addition to these thought-provoking questions, we will also explore some of the most exciting breakthroughs at the frontier of technology. From advanced neural networks that mimic the human brain to quantum computers that promise unparalleled processing power, these technological marvels are not just reshaping the internet but also redefining the very fabric of reality.

As we journey through this narrative, remember: this story is not just about technology. It's about us, our society, our values, and our future. Technology is merely the tool; we are the architects. And with this comes the responsibility to shape the digital world in a way that reflects our shared values and aspirations.

Welcome to the dawn of the sentient web, a realm where human and machine learning intertwine, where data transforms into wisdom, and where the line between the physical and digital blur. As we stand at the cusp of this new era, let's not forget the importance of steering this transformation with wisdom, foresight, and an unwavering commitment to human-centric values. For as we have seen, the internet has evolved from a tool of connectivity to an entity exhibiting sentience. The future - and how we navigate it - is in our hands.

Understanding Artificial Intelligence and Machine Learning

To understand the remarkable transformation of the internet into a near-sentient entity, we need to delve into the heart of the technologies powering it: artificial intelligence (AI) and machine learning (ML). These technologies, once the domain of science fiction, are now an integral part of our daily digital interactions. But what exactly are AI and ML? How do they work, and how do they intermingle to create the Sentient Web?

Artificial intelligence, at its core, is about the development of machines that can perform tasks requiring human-like intelligence. These tasks include learning from experience, understanding natural language, recognizing patterns, and making decisions. AI can be classified into two broad types: Narrow AI and General AI.

Narrow AI, also known as Weak AI, is designed to perform a single task and is the type of AI we interact with most frequently today. When Siri recognizes your voice command or when your email filters spam, it's Narrow AI at work. These AI systems operate under a limited set of constraints and are usually only capable of doing the specific task they were designed for.

General AI, on the other hand, possesses the capacity to understand, learn, adapt, and implement knowledge across a broad range of tasks. This is the type of AI often depicted in movies, an intelligent system that has similar cognitive capabilities to a human being. However, as of the current date, General AI remains a theoretical concept and is still a subject of active research.

AI's evolution has been marked by distinct waves, each characterized by the development of novel techniques to mimic human intelligence. Early attempts at AI in the mid-

20th century focused on rule-based systems where programmers defined explicit rules for the AI to follow. Though these systems could solve complex problems, their intelligence was rigid and inflexible, lacking the capacity to learn and adapt.

That's where machine learning comes in. Machine learning is a subfield of AI that provides systems the ability to learn from data without being explicitly programmed. Instead of writing detailed instructions for every task, ML allows a system to learn from examples, identify patterns, and make predictions. This marked a significant paradigm shift in the field of AI, transforming it from a static, rule-based system to a dynamic, data-driven one.

At the heart of ML are algorithms - a set of mathematical instructions that guide the learning process. These algorithms vary in complexity and are tailored to different types of tasks. For example, a type of ML algorithm known as regression might be used to predict housing prices based on historical data, while a classification algorithm might be used to distinguish spam emails from legitimate ones.
There are three primary types of machine learning: supervised learning, unsupervised learning, and reinforcement learning.

Supervised learning involves training an algorithm with labeled data, where both the inputs and the desired outputs are provided. The algorithm learns a mapping from inputs to outputs and can then apply this learning to new, unseen data.

Unsupervised learning, in contrast, deals with unlabeled data. The algorithm is given a dataset and tasked with finding patterns or structure within this data, such as grouping customers based on their purchasing behavior.

Reinforcement learning is about learning from interaction with an environment. Here, an agent learns to make decisions by taking actions, receiving rewards or penalties, and adjusting its behavior accordingly. This type of learning is commonly used in autonomous vehicles and game-playing AI.

Machine learning, with its ability to sift through vast amounts of data and learn from it, has propelled AI from a theoretical concept to a practical, powerful tool. It's the engine driving our personalized online experiences, our digital assistants, our recommendation systems, and much more. But as we'll explore later, the power of machine learning is not without its pitfalls.

However, ML is just one piece of the AI puzzle. To create truly intelligent systems, other components, like natural language processing, speech recognition, and computer vision, also come into play.

Natural language processing (NLP) enables machines to understand, generate, and respond in human language, bridging the communication gap between humans and computers. It's the reason Siri can understand your requests, and Google Translate can translate text into different languages.

Speech recognition is a subset of NLP, focusing on transforming spoken language into written form. It's the technology behind voice-activated systems like Amazon's Alexa or Google Home.

Computer vision is about enabling machines to see and understand visual information from the environment, analogous to human vision. It's used in a wide range of applications, from facial recognition systems to self-driving cars.

Integrating these components with machine learning creates AI systems that can interact with the world in increasingly human-like ways, driving the evolution of the sentient web.

Now, you might be wondering: if these systems can learn and adapt, does that mean they think like us? The answer is both yes and no. While these systems can mimic certain aspects of human intelligence, they don't possess consciousness or self-awareness. They don't have beliefs, desires, fears, or ambitions. They don't understand context in the way humans do, and they can't extrapolate knowledge to areas outside their training data. At least, not yet.

As of our current understanding, AI and ML are powerful tools that can process vast amounts of data, identify patterns, and make predictions, but they are still tools. They operate within the boundaries of their design and programming, no matter how sophisticated that may be.

However, this doesn't diminish their impact. The integration of AI and ML into the internet has been transformative, enabling a level of personalization, interactivity, and responsiveness that was unimaginable a few decades ago. From AI chatbots that provide customer service, to recommendation algorithms that curate personalized content, to predictive analytics that drive business decisions, AI and ML are reshaping our digital landscape.

But, like any transformative technology, they present unique challenges. These include data privacy concerns, algorithmic bias, the digital divide, and the potential for misuse. As these technologies continue to evolve and become more embedded in our lives, it's crucial to navigate these challenges with care, ensuring that the benefits of AI and ML are realized while mitigating their potential risks.

As we continue our journey through the world of the sentient web, we will delve deeper into these challenges, and the ethical considerations they raise. We will explore the intersection of technology and society, the balance of innovation and regulation, and the role of human agency in an increasingly automated world.

In the grand tapestry of the sentient web, AI and ML are the threads weaving together a complex, dynamic, and ever-evolving digital ecosystem. Understanding these technologies, their capabilities, and their limitations, is key to navigating our data-driven era and shaping the future of the internet.

Cognitive Computing: The Brain of the Sentient Web

As we delve deeper into the intricacies of the Sentient Web, it's crucial to understand one of the most powerful forces behind this digital revolution: cognitive computing. Cognitive computing, often perceived as the brain of the sentient web, is the simulation of human thought processes in a computerized model. It involves self-learning systems that use machine learning techniques to perform tasks traditionally requiring human intelligence.

Cognitive computing draws from a variety of disciplines, including artificial intelligence (AI), machine learning (ML), natural language processing (NLP), and more. Its ultimate goal is not just to develop systems that are intelligent but to create ones that are capable of understanding, reasoning, learning, and interacting in ways similar to the human brain.

Let's unravel the complex world of cognitive computing and see how it forms the foundation of the sentient web.

Understanding Cognitive Computing

Cognitive computing is about creating machines that mimic the way the human brain works. It's not just about processing power or crunching numbers at lightning speed; it's about systems that can understand, reason, and learn from their interactions with humans and the environment.

At the heart of cognitive computing are technologies we've already discussed: AI and ML. These technologies enable systems to learn from experience, adapt to new situations, understand natural language, and make decisions. However, cognitive computing takes this a step further by attempting to mimic the way the human brain works.

The human brain is an incredibly complex and efficient processor. It can process vast amounts of information, make connections between disparate pieces of data, understand context, and adapt to changing situations. It's this ability to understand, reason, and learn that cognitive computing strives to replicate.

Cognitive systems are designed to learn and interact naturally with people, extend and magnify human expertise, and sift through vast amounts of data to provide insights and enhance decision-making.

Components of Cognitive Computing

Cognitive computing combines several components to create systems that can understand, reason, and learn. These components include machine learning, natural language processing, data mining, and human-computer interaction.

Machine Learning: As we've discussed, ML is a type of AI that provides systems the ability to learn from data without being explicitly programmed. Cognitive systems use ML algorithms to learn from interactions, identify patterns, and make predictions.

Natural Language Processing: NLP enables machines to understand and respond in human language. Cognitive systems use NLP to interact naturally with users, understand context, and draw insights from unstructured data like text or speech.

Data Mining: Data mining is the process of discovering patterns in large datasets. Cognitive systems use data mining techniques to sift through vast amounts of data, identifying patterns and trends that can inform decision-making.

Human-Computer Interaction: This component is about creating systems that are easy and intuitive for humans to use. Cognitive systems should be able to understand and respond to human input in a way that feels natural and intuitive.

These components are integrated into a cohesive system that can understand, reason, and learn from its interactions with the world. This makes cognitive computing a driving force behind the sentient web.

Cognitive Computing in Action

Cognitive computing is already making its presence felt in various industries and fields. For example, in healthcare, cognitive systems can analyze patient data, medical literature, and clinical guidelines to provide personalized treatment recommendations. These systems can also assist in research, sifting through vast amounts of scientific literature to identify relevant studies or uncover new insights.

In the business world, cognitive computing can enhance decision-making by analyzing market trends, customer behavior, and internal data to provide actionable insights. It can also improve customer service by understanding and responding to customer queries in natural language.

In the realm of the Sentient Web, cognitive computing is behind intelligent personal assistants that understand your voice commands, social media algorithms that curate personalized content, and recommendation systems that suggest products or media based on your preferences.

These applications are just the tip of the iceberg. As cognitive computing continues to evolve, its potential applications are virtually limitless.

The Future of Cognitive Computing and the Sentient Web

Looking forward, cognitive computing promises to play a pivotal role in the evolution of the Sentient Web. As these systems become more sophisticated, we can expect a web that is not just responsive, but proactive, capable of understanding our needs, preferences, and behaviors, and adapting to them in real-time.

Imagine a digital assistant that doesn't just respond to your commands, but anticipates your needs, providing information or performing tasks before you even ask. Or a search engine that understands your queries in the same way a human would, providing more relevant and context-aware results.

These are not far-off fantasies, but real possibilities that cognitive computing can make possible. As these systems become more integrated into our daily lives, they have the potential to transform the way we interact with the web, making it more intuitive, personalized, and intelligent.

Ethical Considerations

However, this brave new world of cognitive computing is not without its challenges. As we've touched on before, the increasing intelligence of our digital systems raises a number of ethical and societal questions.

Data privacy is a major concern, as cognitive systems rely on vast amounts of data to function effectively. How do we ensure that this data is collected, stored, and used in a way that respects individual privacy and autonomy? How do we balance the benefits of personalized, intelligent services with the need to protect personal information?

Algorithmic bias is another challenge. If cognitive systems are trained on biased data, they can perpetuate and amplify these biases in their decisions and recommendations. Ensuring that these systems are fair, transparent, and accountable is a critical task.

There's also the question of human agency in an increasingly automated world. As cognitive systems take over tasks traditionally performed by humans, what role do we play? How do we ensure that these systems enhance human capabilities rather than replace them?

These questions, among others, will be the focus of our ongoing exploration of the Sentient Web. As we journey through this complex and fascinating landscape, we must remember that technology is a tool, shaped by our values, our choices, and our actions. The future of the Sentient Web, and the role of cognitive computing in it, is in our hands.

Cognitive computing is more than just a technological advancement; it's a new way of interacting with the digital world, one that promises to make the web more intuitive, personalized, and intelligent. It's the brain of the Sentient Web, driving its evolution and shaping its future.

By understanding it, we can better navigate the challenges and opportunities of our data-driven era and shape the future of the internet in a way that benefits all. As we continue our exploration of the Sentient Web, we will delve deeper into these challenges and the ethical considerations they raise, exploring the intersection of technology, society, and human agency.

The journey is as complex and intriguing as the destination, so stay with us as we journey through the ever-evolving landscape of the Sentient Web.

Case Study: The Rise of Smart Technology and the Internet of Things

In this section, we'll explore a pivotal development in the digital transformation shaping our world: the rise of smart technology and the Internet of Things (IoT). By examining this technological evolution, we can gain a deeper understanding of the Sentient Web's vast interconnected landscape, its growing impact on our daily lives, and the ethical implications it brings to light.

Understanding Smart Technology and the IoT

At its simplest, smart technology refers to devices or systems that can make decisions and perform tasks without human intervention. These devices can adapt to their environments, learn from experience, and interact with other devices, all while generating and analyzing vast amounts of data.

The Internet of Things (IoT), a key component of smart technology, is a vast network of interconnected devices that communicate and exchange data. It ranges from everyday objects like smartphones and home appliances, to industrial machinery, healthcare devices, and even entire cities. This broad spectrum of connectivity is transforming the way we live and work.

The Journey from Connected Devices to Smart Technology

The first inklings of the IoT emerged in the late 20th century, when the idea of connecting physical devices to the internet started gaining traction. This began with computers and eventually expanded to mobile phones, giving birth to the idea of "always-on" connectivity.
However, the real turning point came with the proliferation of sensors and wireless technology.

Suddenly, it wasn't just computers and phones that could connect to the internet, but everyday devices from refrigerators to thermostats. These devices could now gather data about their environment, communicate with each other, and even respond to changes autonomously.

Smart technology took this concept a step further, introducing devices that could not just connect and communicate, but also learn and adapt. Powered by advances in AI and machine learning, these devices can analyze the data they collect, identify patterns, make predictions, and adjust their behavior accordingly.

The Impact of Smart Technology and the IoT

The rise of smart technology and the IoT has profound implications for various sectors of society, reshaping industries, public services, and our personal lives.

In Industry: The industrial internet of things (IIoT) is revolutionizing manufacturing, logistics, and supply chain management. Sensors monitor equipment performance and predict maintenance needs, autonomous robots streamline production lines, and smart logistics solutions optimize supply chains. The result is increased efficiency, cost savings, and improved product quality.

In Healthcare: IoT devices, such as wearable fitness trackers and remote patient monitoring systems, gather health data for personalized care. AI-powered analysis of this data can predict health risks and facilitate early intervention. Telehealth platforms enable remote consultations, improving access to healthcare services.

In Smart Cities: IoT technology is making cities smarter, safer, and more sustainable. Sensors monitor environmental conditions and traffic patterns, improving urban planning. Smart grids optimize energy use, reducing environmental impact. Public safety is enhanced through surveillance systems and emergency response solutions.

In Homes: Smart homes are no longer a futuristic concept. From smart thermostats that adjust temperature based on user patterns, to voice-activated assistants that control home appliances, smart technology is making homes more comfortable, convenient, and energy-efficient.

The Role of Smart Technology in the Sentient Web

The rise of smart technology and the IoT is a key driver of the Sentient Web. These interconnected, intelligent devices form the nodes of the Sentient Web, continuously generating, analyzing, and responding to data. The Sentient Web is thus not just a network of interconnected devices, but an intelligent, evolving ecosystem that learns from and adapts to its interactions with humans and the environment.

Navigating the Challenges

However, as with any revolutionary technology, the rise of smart technology and the IoT brings its own set of challenges. For one, there's the issue of data privacy and security. IoT devices generate vast amounts of data, often of a personal or sensitive nature. Ensuring this data is collected, stored, and used in a way that respects user privacy and secures it from potential cyber threats is a significant challenge.

Interoperability is another issue. With a vast array of IoT devices from different manufacturers, ensuring these devices can communicate and work together effectively is not always straightforward. Standardization of protocols and interfaces is a critical aspect of this challenge.

Additionally, there's the challenge of digital divide. While smart technology has the potential to make our lives easier and more efficient, there's a risk that those without access to such technology could be left behind, exacerbating existing social and economic inequalities.

Looking Ahead

Despite these challenges, the rise of smart technology and the IoT is an exciting development in our digital evolution, one that holds immense potential. As we move towards an increasingly data-driven world, the Sentient Web – powered by interconnected, intelligent devices – will play a pivotal role in shaping our future.

Imagine a future where your smart home knows when you're about to arrive and adjusts the temperature, lighting, and even music to your preference. Your fridge automatically orders groceries when they're running low, and your car drives you to work while you catch up on news or emails. On a larger scale, imagine smart cities that optimize resources, reduce environmental impact, and improve the quality of life for their inhabitants.

These scenarios may seem like science fiction, but they are rapidly becoming reality thanks to the rise of smart technology and the IoT. As these technologies continue to evolve, they promise to make the Sentient Web more intuitive, responsive, and attuned to our needs.

However, as we embrace these technologies, it's essential to navigate their challenges responsibly. Balancing the benefits of smart technology with ethical considerations of privacy, security, interoperability, and equity will be critical in shaping a future where technology serves humanity, not the other way around.

In the coming chapters, we will explore these challenges in more depth, along with potential strategies to address them. As we journey further into the Sentient Web, we'll see that it's not just about the technology, but about how we use it – how we balance the incredible potential of these tools with the responsibility to use them wisely and ethically.

The rise of smart technology and the IoT marks a significant milestone in our journey towards the Sentient Web. By understanding this evolution, we can better navigate the challenges and opportunities of our data-driven era, shaping the future of the internet in a way that benefits all.

This journey is as complex as it is fascinating, and we invite you to join us as we continue to explore the contours of the Sentient Web.

Chapter 2: Human and Machine Agency in the Digital Age

Human Agency in an Automated World

As we delve further into our discussion of the sentient web and the landscape of artificial intelligence, we must confront one of the central conundrums of this new digital age: the paradox of human agency in an increasingly automated world.

Human agency refers to the capacity of individuals to act independently, to make their free choices, and to shape their own lives. It's a vital aspect of our human experience, deeply intertwined with our sense of identity, autonomy, and purpose. But as machines become more intelligent and automation permeates various facets of our lives, what happens to this human agency?

Confronting the Automation Paradox

At the surface level, automation seems to undermine human agency. If machines are performing tasks, making decisions, and even learning on their own, where does that leave us? Do we merely become passive recipients of automated services and decisions, spectators in a world run by machines?

This perspective, often associated with dystopian narratives, paints a grim picture of human obsolescence. However, it misses a crucial nuance. Automation doesn't necessarily diminish human agency; it transforms it. It changes the ways in which we exercise our agency, the spaces in which we do so, and the tools we use in the process.

Redefining Agency in an Automated World

In an automated world, our agency is not simply about doing, but about guiding. It's about setting goals, defining values, and shaping the contexts within which machines operate. It's about deciding what we automate and why, how we design and use AI systems, and how we navigate the social, ethical, and existential implications of these technologies.

Take the example of a self-driving car. On one hand, the car's automation might seem to curtail your agency—you're not physically driving the car. But on another level, it could enhance your agency. You choose the destination, the route, the speed. You decide when to use the self-driving mode and when to override it. You're not controlling the vehicle's every movement, but you're guiding its overall journey.

This highlights a key aspect of human agency in an automated world: our role as decision-makers, designers, and stewards. We're not just users of automated systems; we're their creators and regulators. Our agency lies in our ability to design machines that reflect our values, to set the rules and boundaries within which they operate, and to ensure that they serve our individual and collective needs.

Navigating the Agency-Automation Nexus

In this context, our challenge is not merely to preserve human agency amidst automation, but to redefine it. To recognize that our agency is not threatened by machines, but is intertwined with them. That our relationship with machines is not zero-sum (where one's gain is another's loss), but symbiotic. And that our task is not to resist automation, but to navigate its possibilities and pitfalls, to steer its course in a way that reflects our human aspirations.

We're not just navigating the landscapes of the sentient web; we're shaping them. We're not just adapting to automation; we're defining its meaning and purpose. And we're not just preserving our agency; we're transforming it, cultivating a form of agency that is attuned to the complexities of our automated world, that recognizes our interdependence with machines, and that seeks to shape our technological trajectory in a way that enhances our humanity, not diminishes it.

In this journey, we'll encounter challenges and dilemmas. We'll grapple with questions of control and freedom, of identity and obsolescence, of purpose and meaning. But in doing so, we'll also discover new ways of being, thinking, and acting. We'll cultivate a new form of agency—an 'augmented' agency—that leverages the power of automation to enhance our capabilities, expand our horizons, and deepen our humanity.

The Rise of Augmented Agency

Augmented agency doesn't imply the surrendering of our autonomy to machines, but rather its amplification. It involves using AI and automation as tools to extend our capacities, to reach beyond our limitations, and to create new possibilities for action, creation, and impact.

Consider how AI can augment our decision-making. By processing vast amounts of data and detecting patterns beyond human reach, AI can offer insights that enrich our understanding and inform our decisions. Yet it's still us, humans, who interpret these insights, contextualize them, and decide how to act upon them. The AI doesn't replace our decision-making; it augments it.

Similarly, consider how automation can augment our productivity. Automated systems can perform routine tasks more efficiently, accurately, and tirelessly than humans. This frees us from mundane work and offers us more time and energy for creative, strategic, and interpersonal tasks—the tasks that require human ingenuity, judgment, and empathy. Automation doesn't make us redundant; it makes us indispensable.

In these ways and more, AI and automation can serve as extensions of our agency, not threats to it. They can enable us to see deeper, reach further, and act smarter. They can empower us to tackle complex problems, to pursue bold visions, and to create meaningful change. They can help us to not just survive in the digital age, but to thrive in it.

The Ethics of Augmented Agency

Yet, cultivating this augmented agency isn't merely a technical endeavor; it's an ethical one. It demands that we consider not just how we can augment our agency, but why, for whom, and at what cost.

We must ensure that the benefits of augmented agency are accessible to all, not just a privileged few. We must consider the potential downsides of augmented agency, such as privacy risks, bias in AI systems, or the psychological effects of increased dependence on machines. And we must keep asking what it means to be human in an automated world, how we can preserve our human dignity, diversity, and spirit in the face of technological change.

Augmented Agency: A New Frontier

In the end, the rise of the sentient web doesn't signal the end of human agency, but its evolution. It heralds the birth of a new form of agency—a form that is deeply intertwined with machines, that harnesses the power of automation, and that holds the potential to redefine our relationship with technology and with ourselves.

As we venture into this new frontier, let's remember that we are not just inhabitants of the digital age, but its creators. We are not just subjects of automation, but its architects. We are not just users of the sentient web, but its weavers.

In the face of automation, let's not diminish our agency, but augment it. Let's not resist our symbiosis with machines, but embrace it. And let's not fear the future, but shape it—a future where humans and machines coexist, collaborate, and co-evolve, where technology augments our humanity, and where our agency shines brighter than ever in the heart of the sentient web.

Defining Machine Agency: From Programming to Autonomous Decision Making

As we venture further into our exploration of the digital age, it becomes necessary to shed light on the counterpoint to human agency: machine agency. While human agency is something we intrinsically understand, machine agency represents a new and evolving concept that is fundamentally reshaping our world. But what exactly is machine agency?

Machine Agency: An Evolving Concept

At its most basic, machine agency can be thought of as the ability of machines to take actions or make decisions independently. This independence is not absolute, but it is contextual. It is framed within the boundaries set by human designers and governed by the machine's programming and learning capabilities.

In the early days of computing, machine agency was almost entirely deterministic. Machines were instructed to follow rigid sets of rules and to make decisions based on predefined inputs. They were tools, extensions of human agency that were completely reliant on human inputs and programming to function.

However, as computing technology advanced, particularly with the advent of machine learning and AI, the concept of machine agency began to expand and evolve.

From Programming to Autonomous Decision Making

Machine learning, a subset of artificial intelligence, has greatly broadened the scope of machine agency. These systems are capable of learning from data, making predictions, and updating their models without explicit human instruction. They move beyond rigid programming to draw conclusions and make decisions based on patterns and trends they detect in data.

With deep learning, a subfield of machine learning inspired by the structure and function of the human brain, machines can even learn to recognize complex patterns in massive amounts of data. They can classify images, recognize speech, and even generate human-like text. These systems display a level of agency that is far beyond mere rule-following.

But what distinguishes this form of agency from human agency is its lack of understanding, consciousness, or intentionality. Machines don't have beliefs or desires. They don't understand the meaning or purpose of their actions. They don't experience emotions or have a sense of self. Their agency is purely functional—a product of algorithms, not consciousness.

The Ethical Implications of Machine Agency

The rise of machine agency presents significant ethical questions. As machines take on more responsibilities and make more decisions, we must grapple with the question of accountability. If an AI system makes a decision that leads to harm, who is responsible? The machine, the programmers, the users, or the company that deployed it?

There's also the issue of transparency. As machine learning models become more complex, their decision-making processes can become harder to understand, even for their creators. This lack of transparency, often referred to as the "black box" problem, can make it difficult to understand why a machine made a particular decision or prediction.

Moreover, as machines gain more agency, we must also consider their potential impact on human agency. Will they augment human capabilities and free us from mundane tasks, as we discussed in the previous section? Or will they replace human jobs and decision-making, leading to social and economic disruption?

These ethical considerations underscore the importance of human oversight and control in the development and deployment of AI systems. They remind us that machine agency should not replace human agency, but complement it. And they highlight the need for clear legal and ethical frameworks to guide the growth of machine agency in our increasingly automated world.

Machine Agency: A New Frontier

In summary, machine agency has evolved from simple, deterministic programming to complex, autonomous decision-making. It is a form of functional agency, born of algorithms and data, that lacks the intentionality, understanding, and consciousness of human agency.

As machine agency continues to evolve, it is shaping our world in profound ways—transforming our economies, societies, and cultures; challenging our ethical norms and legal systems; and altering our perceptions of what it means to be agents in an increasingly automated world.

Ethics, Accountability, and Governance

As our world becomes more populated by machines that have the ability to act, the traditional ways in which we have thought about responsibility, accountability, and governance are being disrupted. We can no longer simply assign blame or credit to a human operator when a machine makes a mistake or achieves something remarkable. We need to develop new ways of conceptualizing responsibility and accountability in the age of machine agency.

For example, should we treat AI systems as legal entities that can be held accountable for their actions? Some have suggested the concept of "electronic personhood" for advanced AI, where AI systems would be held accountable in the same way corporations are. This raises additional questions about the rights and protections such systems would have, and how we could enforce accountability.

Alternatively, accountability could be distributed across the various actors involved in the creation, deployment, and use of AI systems. This includes the designers who program the AI, the decision-makers who deploy it, and the users who interact with it. This kind of distributed accountability could ensure that human actors remain responsible for the machines they create and use, but it also complicates the task of identifying who is responsible when things go wrong.

These questions don't have easy answers, and they demand thoughtful dialogue and rigorous research across disciplines. Legal scholars, ethicists, computer scientists, and policy makers must work together to develop new ethical frameworks and governance models for machine agency. These frameworks should promote transparency, accountability, and fairness, while also fostering innovation and progress in AI technology.

The Future of Machine Agency

The evolution of machine agency is far from over. With advances in AI and machine learning, machines are likely to exhibit higher levels of autonomy and complexity in their actions and decision-making. They may become better at understanding and responding to human emotions, needs, and intentions, and they may develop more sophisticated ways of learning and adapting to their environments.

These advancements will bring new opportunities, but also new challenges. They will enable machines to contribute more to our society, economy, and daily lives, but they will also increase the risks of error, abuse, and harm. They will make it more important, and more difficult, to ensure that machine agency serves human agency, rather than undermining it.

In this journey, we must remember that the goal of technology is to enhance human life, not to replace it. We must ensure that as machines gain more agency, humans don't lose theirs. We must strive to create a future where humans and machines are partners, not adversaries—a future where technology is a tool of human empowerment, not a source of human alienation.

This is the challenge, and the promise, of machine agency in the digital age. It is a new frontier of discovery, innovation, and impact—one that requires our deepest attention, our best ideas, and our boldest dreams. As we explore this frontier, let's remember to keep our human values at the center of our technological advances, and to use machine agency to augment, not diminish, our human agency. The sentient web is not just about intelligent machines; it's about wiser humans, too.

Human-Machine Interaction: Cooperation, Co-creation, or Conflict?

Human-Machine Interaction (HMI), the field of study concerned with how humans engage with machines and vice versa, is an integral part of the sentient web. It investigates how humans and machines can efficiently cooperate, creating synergistic relationships, while also addressing potential conflicts that might arise as technology progresses.

From Early Human-Machine Interaction to the Modern Age

The history of HMI is as old as the history of tools. Early humans interacting with simple tools, like a hammer or a wheel, represented the first steps in human-machine interaction. As our tools have grown more sophisticated, so too has our interaction with them. Fast forward to the dawn of computers, and the discipline of Human-Computer Interaction (HCI) emerged, pioneering ways to make these novel machines more user-friendly.

With the advent of the internet, HCI evolved into a more complex form of HMI, focusing not only on individual computers but also on networks of interconnected devices. And now, with the sentient web, we're taking the next step: exploring how humans can interact with AI and other advanced technologies, transforming mere user-friendliness into meaningful, cooperative relationships.

Cooperation and Co-creation in the Sentient Web

One of the key themes in contemporary HMI is cooperation: designing systems that can work effectively with human users, understanding their needs and goals, and helping them achieve those goals. For instance, virtual assistants like Siri or Alexa strive to understand and execute human commands, providing information or performing tasks on our behalf.

But the sentient web aims to take this cooperation to the next level. It envisions AI systems that don't just follow our commands, but can anticipate our needs, understand our emotions, and make decisions in our best interest. It imagines a future where humans and machines are partners, each contributing their unique strengths to achieve shared objectives.

This vision goes beyond cooperation to co-creation: humans and machines working together to create new knowledge, solve complex problems, and invent new possibilities. An example of this is generative AI, where AI systems generate new ideas, designs, or stories, and humans refine and direct these outputs. This symbiosis of human and machine intelligence can potentially unlock unprecedented levels of creativity and innovation.

Conflict and Contention in the Machine Age

While cooperation and co-creation are the aspirational goals of HMI, they are not without challenges. As machines gain more capabilities and agency, conflicts between humans and machines are likely to occur.

These conflicts can take many forms. For instance, there could be disagreements between a human and an AI system over the best course of action. Or, an AI system might make a decision that its human user finds unexpected, confusing, or unethical.

Then there's the broader societal conflict: the fear of machines taking over jobs, leading to economic displacement and social unrest. And the ethical dilemmas: how to balance the benefits of AI with concerns about privacy, fairness, and autonomy.

These are serious concerns that require serious attention. As we develop more advanced and autonomous machines, we must also develop ways to manage these conflicts, to ensure that the rise of machine agency doesn't undermine human well-being.

Towards a Harmonious Human-Machine Symbiosis

The question is not whether humans and machines will interact; they already do, and this interaction will only intensify in the sentient web. The question is how they will interact. Will it be a relationship of cooperation and co-creation, or one of conflict and contention?

The answer depends on how we design our technologies and our societies. If we design them with human values in mind, we can foster a harmonious symbiosis where humans and machines work together for mutual benefit. If we ignore these values or allow them to be trampled in the rush for technological advancement, we may end up in a world of conflict and dissatisfaction. This highlights the importance of fields like AI ethics and values-in-design.

Efforts are underway to integrate ethics and human values into AI systems. For example, the concept of "value alignment" suggests designing AI systems whose goals are aligned with human values. There are also ongoing research and discussions about "explainable AI," AI systems that can explain their reasoning and decisions to human users in understandable terms. These initiatives can help mitigate the risk of conflict and facilitate smoother cooperation between humans and machines.

Meanwhile, on the societal level, it's important to have inclusive discussions about the role of AI and other technologies in our lives. These discussions should not be limited to technologists and policymakers but should include diverse voices from all walks of life. Public deliberation can help shape the direction of technological development and ensure that it benefits all of society, not just a privileged few.

Augmenting Human Capabilities, Not Replacing Them

As we navigate the complexities of human-machine interaction in the sentient web, it's crucial to remember one guiding principle: machines are here to augment human capabilities, not replace them. As the famous computer scientist J.C.R. Licklider noted in his seminal 1960 paper "Man-Computer Symbiosis", the aim is to "enable men and computers to cooperate in making decisions and controlling complex situations without inflexible dependence on predetermined programs."

While it's true that machines are becoming more capable and autonomous, they still lack the rich understanding, creativity, and empathy that are distinctively human. AI can sift through vast amounts of data faster than any human, but it's the human who brings meaning and context to that data. A self-driving car can navigate the roads, but it's the human who enjoys the journey and the scenery.

By focusing on the augmentation rather than replacement, we can imagine a future where humans and machines each contribute their unique strengths to create a more prosperous, inclusive, and fulfilling world. That's the promise of the sentient web, and the future of human-machine interaction.

A Future Shaped by Our Choices

As we stand at the dawn of the sentient web, we have a choice to make. We can choose to build a future where humans and machines work together in a spirit of cooperation and co-creation, enhancing our capabilities and expanding our possibilities. Or we can choose a path where humans and machines are in conflict, with machines dominating or displacing human agency.

Ultimately, the future of human-machine interaction will be shaped not just by technological advances, but by our values, our decisions, and our collective will. It's a future we all have a stake in, and a future we all have a role in creating.

Technological Singularity: Promise or Peril?

The concept of technological singularity has been a hot topic in technology and AI circles, provoking heated debates and thoughtful conversations. It is, in essence, the hypothetical future moment when artificial intelligence will surpass human intelligence and trigger an unimaginable revolution in human civilization. Some look upon this event with excited anticipation, seeing it as the next great leap in our evolutionary journey. Others view it with deep unease, fearing that superintelligent machines could pose an existential threat to humanity. As we venture deeper into the uncharted waters of the sentient web, we must grapple with the profound implications of the technological singularity.

Defining Technological Singularity

The term "singularity" originates from astrophysics, where it describes a point in space-time where the rules of the known universe break down, such as within a black hole. In the context of technology, the singularity signifies a point of unimaginable change, a point beyond which the future becomes hard to predict because of the impact of superintelligent AI.

Futurist and author Ray Kurzweil, a leading proponent of the singularity concept, predicts that this event will occur around 2045. He envisions that technological progress, particularly in AI, will become so rapid and so profound that it will completely transform human life. According to Kurzweil, superintelligent AI will create abundant wealth, cure diseases, extend our lifespans, and enable us to transcend our biological limitations.

On the other hand, some AI researchers and philosophers caution that the singularity could be perilous. If not handled properly, superintelligent AI could pose serious risks, including the existential risk of human extinction. They argue that ensuring the safety and alignment of superintelligent AI is one of the most critical tasks of our time.

Promise: A Leap into Posthuman Era

For those who embrace the singularity, the promise is enticing. They see it as the doorway to a posthuman era, where we can augment our bodies and minds, extend our lifespans, and create a post-scarcity society with unlimited wealth and resources.

AI, according to this perspective, will help us unlock the secrets of biology and conquer diseases that have plagued humanity for centuries. Superintelligent AI could also accelerate scientific discoveries, solve complex problems, and help us understand and tackle global challenges like climate change.

Furthermore, with the advent of superintelligent AI, we could enhance our cognitive abilities and emotional capacities, and even explore other forms of consciousness. It could also open up new realms of experience and creativity, and new ways of relating to each other and the world.

Peril: Existential Risks and Ethical Dilemmas

While the potential benefits of the singularity are immense, so are the risks. A major concern is that superintelligent AI could become uncontrollable. If an AI system becomes much smarter than humans, it could take actions that humans might not anticipate or be able to counter. This could lead to disastrous consequences, particularly if the AI's goals are not perfectly aligned with human values.

The challenge of aligning AI with human values, often referred to as the "alignment problem," is a central issue in AI safety research. Even if we can encode our values into AI, there's the question of whose values should be represented. With cultural variations and evolving societal norms, encoding a universally acceptable set of ethics into an AI might be an insurmountable task.

Another risk is the societal disruption that could come with the singularity. The rise of superintelligent AI could exacerbate inequality, as those with access to advanced technology could become vastly more powerful than others. It could also lead to job displacement and economic upheaval on a scale far beyond what we've seen in the past. This could create social and political instability and widen the gap between the haves and have-nots.

There are also deeper philosophical and existential questions that the singularity brings to the fore. What does it mean to be human in a world where machines outstrip us in intelligence? How do we find purpose and meaning in a world where many of our tasks and challenges have been taken over by machines? And what happens to our sense of self and identity if we start merging with machines, as some singularity proponents suggest?

Navigating the Road to Singularity

Despite these challenges and uncertainties, the singularity is not a foregone conclusion. The timeline and trajectory of AI development are still uncertain and depend on many factors, including scientific breakthroughs, resource availability, and societal decisions.

As we navigate the road to singularity, it's essential to have open, inclusive, and informed discussions about the potential risks and benefits. We need to engage a broad range of stakeholders, including AI researchers, ethicists, policymakers, and the public, to shape the development and deployment of AI in a way that benefits humanity as a whole.

We must also invest in AI safety research to solve the alignment problem and ensure that AI systems behave in ways that are beneficial to humans. And we must prepare for the societal changes that AI could bring, by promoting equitable access to technology, providing education and training for the jobs of the future, and creating social safety nets for those who might be displaced by automation.

Finally, we need to foster a culture of responsibility in the AI community. AI developers and companies should adhere to ethical guidelines and be held accountable for the societal impacts of their technologies. And we, as a society, need to think carefully about the kind of future we want to create and make deliberate choices to steer technology in that direction.

The technological singularity is a fascinating concept that captures the imagination and provokes deep thought about our future. It presents both immense promise and daunting perils. While we can't predict the future with certainty, we can shape it.

By grappling with the ethical implications, investing in safety research, and engaging in thoughtful dialogue, we can navigate the path to the singularity and beyond, in a way that upholds our shared values and advances the common good.

The sentience of the web, far from being a threat, can become an opportunity to amplify our collective intelligence and create a more prosperous, equitable, and sustainable world.

In the end, the future of AI and the sentient web is not just about technology, but about us, about our choices, and about the kind of world we want to create.

Chapter 3: The Big Data Revolution

Big Data and the Sentient Web: An Inextricable Connection

In our contemporary digital age, data has taken center stage, driving transformations across industries and shaping our lives in ways we are only beginning to understand. The rise of big data – massive datasets that can be mined for information and insights – has been both a product of and a catalyst for the development of the sentient web. Big data and the sentient web are indeed inextricably linked, feeding into each other in a continuous loop of growth and evolution. This chapter offers a deep dive into this connection, exploring how big data fuels the sentient web and how, in turn, the sentient web amplifies the power and potential of big data.

The Rise of Big Data

The term "big data" has emerged in the last decade to refer to datasets so large and complex that traditional data processing methods are insufficient to handle them. The explosion of big data has been driven by several key trends. First, the proliferation of digital devices and the internet has led to an unprecedented surge in data generation. Every minute, millions of emails are sent, millions of searches are made on Google, thousands of photos are shared on Instagram, and hundreds of hours of video are uploaded to YouTube. Moreover, the rise of the Internet of Things (IoT) means that an increasing number of objects – from cars and refrigerators to watches and thermostats – are connected to the internet and continuously generating data.

Second, advances in storage and processing technologies have made it feasible and cost-effective to collect, store, and analyze these vast amounts of data. Cloud computing, in particular, has provided scalable, on-demand storage and computing resources, making big data accessible to businesses of all sizes.

Third, there has been a growing recognition of the value of data as a strategic asset. Companies and organizations have come to realize that by analyzing big data, they can gain valuable insights, make more informed decisions, and create new products and services.

Big Data and the Birth of the Sentient Web

Big data has been instrumental in the birth of the sentient web. The fundamental premise of the sentient web – a web that learns and adapts based on user behavior – relies on having vast amounts of data to learn from. Machine learning algorithms, the engines of the sentient web, are essentially pattern recognition systems. They need large amounts of data to identify patterns, make predictions, and improve performance.

Take the example of a recommendation engine on an e-commerce site. The engine uses data about customers' past purchases and browsing history to predict what products they might be interested in. The more data it has, the more accurate its predictions. Big data provides the raw material that fuels these learning processes and enables the web to become "sentient."

The sentient web, in turn, generates even more data. As users interact with sentient systems, they leave digital footprints that can be collected and analyzed, creating a virtuous cycle of data generation and learning. The sentient web and big data are thus entwined in a symbiotic relationship, each one enabling and amplifying the other.

Big Data Challenges

While big data offers immense opportunities, it also brings several challenges. First, big data can be messy and unstructured, requiring sophisticated tools and techniques to clean, integrate, and analyze. Second, big data often raises privacy and security concerns. As more and more personal information is collected and analyzed, there is a risk of data breaches and misuse of data. These issues require robust data governance and privacy protection measures.

Another significant challenge is the potential for bias and discrimination. If the data used to train machine learning algorithms contains biases – and often it does, reflecting existing social inequalities – these biases can be perpetuated and even amplified by the algorithms. This could lead to unjust outcomes, such as discriminatory hiring practices or unfair loan approvals. Hence, understanding and addressing these biases in big data is a crucial task for researchers and practitioners.

A third challenge lies in the realm of data interpretation. Making sense of big data requires not just technical skills but also critical thinking and domain expertise. There's a danger that people can get caught up in the "data hype" and forget that data does not speak for itself. Interpretation of the data is crucial and often requires deep knowledge of the context and the nature of the data.

Big Data Ethics

As we navigate the big data landscape, ethical considerations are paramount. Who owns the data generated by users? Who has the right to access and use this data? How should benefits derived from data be distributed? These are some of the fundamental questions posed by big data ethics.

Ethics also play a vital role in the handling and processing of personal data. The right to privacy needs to be balanced with the benefits of big data analysis. Consent becomes complex in the era of big data, as it's not always clear what users are consenting to when they provide their data. Moreover, as the Cambridge Analytica scandal showed, there can be severe societal repercussions when personal data is misused.

The Future of Big Data and the Sentient Web

Looking ahead, the interplay between big data and the sentient web will continue to shape the digital landscape. We can expect even more sophisticated algorithms, more personalized services, and more efficient systems.

At the same time, we also need to be aware of the potential risks and challenges. As big data and the sentient web become more entwined with our lives, the decisions they inform will have increasing personal and societal impacts. Hence, we need to develop robust ethical and legal frameworks to guide these developments.

The connection between big data and the sentient web is fundamental to understanding our digital age. Their symbiotic relationship has catalyzed the creation of a new era of the internet, transforming the way we live, work, and interact with the world. By gaining a deep understanding of this relationship and its implications, we can better navigate the challenges and opportunities of the big data revolution.

Privacy in the Age of Big Data: Redefining Data Privacy

As we stride deeper into the age of big data, the concept of privacy is undergoing a profound transformation. Privacy, traditionally associated with solitude and the seclusion of personal matters, is being challenged by the relentless march of technology that thrives on data, connectivity, and sharing. The pervasive nature of digital technologies and the massive trove of data they generate are radically reshaping our understanding of what privacy means in this digital era.

The Erosion of Privacy

In the age of big data, we've grown accustomed to exchanging our personal data for services. Our digital footprints are captured at every click, swipe, and interaction, painting an incredibly detailed portrait of our lives. As this data is stored, shared, and analyzed, it fuels the engines of the sentient web, offering personalized recommendations, targeted ads, and efficient services.

However, this convenience comes at the cost of personal privacy. The line between public and private space is blurred. Our likes and dislikes, health status, financial situation, location, and even our deepest secrets are out in the open, collected and scrutinized.

The Rise of Surveillance Capitalism

This intrusion into our personal lives is being driven, in part, by a new form of capitalism – surveillance capitalism. Surveillance capitalism, a term coined by Shoshana Zuboff, refers to the commodification of personal data. Our personal experiences are translated into data, which are then packaged and sold to the highest bidder.

This model presents a fundamental challenge to privacy. As Zuboff notes, surveillance capitalism "unilaterally claims human experience as free raw material for translation into behavioral data." Consequently, our private experiences, thoughts, and emotions are commodified, ushering in an era of unprecedented surveillance.

Redefining Data Privacy

In this context, privacy needs to be redefined. It's no longer sufficient to think of privacy in terms of seclusion or keeping secrets. Instead, privacy should be understood as the right to control one's personal data, the right to know who is collecting the data, for what purpose, and the right to object or limit such collection.

This view of privacy is known as informational self-determination. It emphasizes the agency and autonomy of individuals in determining the fate of their personal data. In this sense, privacy is more about having control over the information flow, deciding who has access to your data, and how it can be used.

Data Privacy Laws and Regulations

With this new understanding of privacy, there has been a surge of data privacy laws and regulations worldwide. The European Union's General Data Protection Regulation (GDPR) stands as a landmark law in this domain. It strengthens individuals' control over their data, giving them the right to access, rectify, and delete their data.

However, GDPR also highlights the challenges of implementing such regulations. For instance, the requirement to obtain user consent for data collection has resulted in lengthy and complex terms of service agreements that many users accept without fully understanding the implications.

Privacy-Enhancing Technologies

Apart from regulations, technological solutions are also emerging to safeguard privacy in the age of big data. These privacy-enhancing technologies (PETs) aim to protect users' personal data while still allowing for data analysis and use.

For instance, differential privacy is a technique that adds noise to the data to preserve individual privacy while allowing for aggregate analysis. Homomorphic encryption allows for computations on encrypted data without the need for decryption, offering privacy-preserving data analysis. While promising, these technologies are still in their infancy and face challenges in terms of efficiency and practicality.

The Road Ahead: A Balancing Act

Looking ahead, protecting privacy in the age of big data will be a delicate balancing act. On one hand, we have the undeniable benefits of big data analytics and the services it provides. On the other, we have the fundamental right to privacy and autonomy, which is threatened by the unchecked collection and use of personal data.

Technology and regulation must work in tandem to ensure this balance. We need to design systems that respect privacy by default, not as an afterthought. These systems should give users transparency about the data being collected and how it's used. They should also provide meaningful control over their data, allowing users to opt-out without losing access to essential services.

However, redefining data privacy is not solely a technological or legal challenge. It's a societal one. As we collectively navigate this data-driven era, we need to have an open dialogue about what privacy means in the context of the sentient web.

Should we accept privacy loss as the inevitable price for the convenience of digital services? Or should we strive to construct a digital environment where privacy and utility are not at odds? These are not easy questions, and the answers will likely vary across different societies and cultures.

Another critical aspect of this dialogue involves educating the public about data privacy. Understanding how personal data is collected, shared, and used is crucial for individuals to make informed decisions and exercise their right to privacy.

Moreover, it's also essential to involve the public in decision-making processes about data privacy. Whether it's through public consultations for new laws or user involvement in designing privacy settings, giving the public a voice can help ensure that privacy protections align with societal values and expectations.

The age of big data has forced us to reconsider the concept of privacy. As we move forward, we must redefine privacy in a way that reflects our digital reality, respects individual autonomy, and adapts to the evolving symbiosis of human and machine agency. It's a challenging task, no doubt, but one that's essential for the healthy development of the sentient web. The future of our digital world hinges on our ability to navigate this transformation while upholding the values we hold dear. Privacy, redefined and reinforced, will be a cornerstone of this future.

Algorithmic Bias: The Dark Side of Data Analysis

As we delve deeper into the age of big data, one term that continually crops up is 'algorithmic bias.' The issue of bias in AI has garnered significant attention recently, prompting widespread debate and fostering a growing concern in society. To many, the promise of objective, emotionless decision-making machines crumbles when the veil is lifted, revealing biases hidden in the algorithms that underpin these systems. In this section, we will dissect the concept of algorithmic bias, its origins, implications, and how we might mitigate its effects in our data-driven era.

Algorithms are sets of instructions or rules that computers follow to perform tasks. When fed with data, they analyze, learn, predict, and make decisions based on the patterns they find. They are the backbone of machine learning and artificial intelligence, powering the sentient web from behind the scenes.

However, like any tool, algorithms are not intrinsically good or bad. Their value is determined by how they are used and, importantly, the data they are fed. If the data input into an algorithm contains biases, the algorithm will learn, perpetuate, and even exacerbate these biases, leading to skewed outputs. This is where we encounter algorithmic bias.

Origins of Algorithmic Bias

The origins of algorithmic bias are multifaceted, but they essentially boil down to two sources: biased data and biased algorithmic design.

The most common origin is biased data. If the data used to train an AI system is not representative of the population it serves, the system will not perform equitably. For instance, if an AI developed to predict skin cancer is trained mainly on images of light-skinned individuals, its performance on darker-skinned individuals may be poor, potentially leading to misdiagnoses.

The other source of bias stems from the design of the algorithm itself. Algorithms are created by humans, and whether intentionally or not, human biases can seep into the algorithmic design process. If an algorithm is designed to prioritize a specific outcome without considering other relevant factors, it may inadvertently disadvantage certain groups of people.

Implications of Algorithmic Bias

The implications of algorithmic bias are profound and far-reaching. With AI systems being increasingly used in critical areas like healthcare, criminal justice, and employment, biased algorithms can lead to unfair outcomes and perpetuate systemic inequalities.

For example, an AI system used in hiring might unfairly disadvantage women or minority candidates if it was trained on data reflecting a company's past hiring biases. Similarly, a predictive policing system might disproportionately target certain neighborhoods or demographic groups if it was trained on biased crime data. In these scenarios, the consequences of algorithmic bias are not just theoretical—they affect real people's lives and livelihoods.

Mitigating Algorithmic Bias

Mitigating algorithmic bias is a complex task, but it is essential for ensuring the fair and ethical use of AI. It involves numerous steps, including improving data collection and curation, developing fair algorithms, and establishing robust oversight mechanisms.

Improving data collection and curation entails ensuring that the data used to train AI systems are representative of the populations they serve. This might involve collecting more diverse data or applying statistical techniques to correct for known biases in the data.

On the algorithmic design front, researchers are developing 'fair' algorithms that aim to minimize bias. These algorithms incorporate fairness constraints into their learning processes, helping to reduce biased outputs. However, defining what 'fairness' means in a mathematical context is a challenging task and a subject of ongoing research.

Finally, robust oversight mechanisms are needed to monitor AI systems for biased outcomes continually. This might involve regular audits of AI systems or the creation of independent oversight bodies. Transparency is key here; developers should be open about their algorithms' design and the data used to train them, allowing for external review and accountability.

While these measures can help reduce bias, it's essential to recognize that they are not a panacea. Eliminating bias completely may not be feasible, given the complexities of human societies and their inherent inequalities. Instead, the goal should be to understand, acknowledge, and manage these biases to mitigate their adverse impacts.

AI Ethics and the Fight against Bias

The issue of algorithmic bias firmly sits within the broader discussion of AI ethics—a field that seeks to ensure AI and machine learning technologies are developed and used in a way that is just, fair, and respects human rights. It involves examining not just the technical aspects of AI, but also the societal, legal, and philosophical issues surrounding these technologies.

As AI continues to infiltrate every aspect of our lives, a concerted, multidisciplinary effort is needed to address the issue of algorithmic bias. This involves computer scientists, data analysts, ethicists, sociologists, lawmakers, and the general public. Everyone has a stake in the development and use of AI, and everyone should have a voice in shaping its ethical guidelines.

Regulation and Legislation

An important aspect of countering algorithmic bias is the implementation of appropriate regulation and legislation. Given the potential consequences of biased AI decisions, there is a growing call for stricter oversight of AI technologies, particularly those used in high-stakes domains like healthcare or criminal justice.

While crafting effective legislation for rapidly evolving technologies is notoriously difficult, there are promising developments. In many jurisdictions, lawmakers are increasingly recognizing the need for stricter AI regulation and are taking steps to introduce relevant legislation. However, a delicate balance must be struck to ensure that regulatory measures protect against harm without stifling innovation.

Conclusion: A Path Forward

While algorithmic bias is a pressing issue, it's important not to lose sight of the immense potential of AI and machine learning technologies. They have the power to revolutionize countless domains, from healthcare and education to energy and the environment.

The challenge, then, is to harness this potential in a way that benefits all of humanity, without leaving anyone behind. This is no easy task, and there will undoubtedly be hurdles along the way. However, by embracing a spirit of openness, collaboration, and relentless questioning, it is a task that society is fully capable of achieving.

As we navigate the complexities of the big data revolution, let's not forget the fundamental principle that should guide our journey: technology, in all its forms, must be harnessed for the collective good. Whether we're grappling with the intricacies of algorithmic bias, privacy concerns, or the prospect of a sentient web, this principle remains our steadfast compass, lighting the path toward a more equitable, fair, and inclusive digital future.

Cybersecurity: Safeguarding Our Data-Rich Landscape

As our world continues to evolve, so too does the landscape of cybersecurity. The big data revolution and the internet of things have both brought a wealth of opportunities and conveniences. However, they have also ushered in new risks and challenges in protecting our digital infrastructure and personal information. As we gather more data and connect more devices to the internet, we must also escalate our efforts in cybersecurity. Let's delve deeper into this new terrain of digital security in our increasingly interconnected world.

The Changing Face of Cyber Threats

The first step in ensuring effective cybersecurity is to understand the changing face of cyber threats. In the early days of the internet, hackers were often individuals or small groups trying to prove their technical prowess or cause minor disruptions. Today, the world of cybercrime has dramatically evolved and expanded.

Modern cyber threats can come from organized criminal networks, state-sponsored hackers, or even corporate espionage teams. They are equipped with advanced skills and tools, and their motivations range from financial gain to political influence. The nature of their attacks has also broadened. They can steal sensitive information, disrupt essential services, manipulate public opinion, or even sabotage physical infrastructure.

The Complexity of Protecting Big Data

Big data represents a tantalizing target for cyber attackers. With the vast amount of information that big data repositories contain, a successful breach can yield a treasure trove of valuable insights. This could include personal details, financial information, health records, business strategies, or state secrets.

Securing big data is inherently challenging due to its characteristics. Its vast volume means that traditional security measures might not be sufficient or scalable. The variety of data types, from structured databases to unstructured social media posts, also complicates the implementation of comprehensive security measures. Furthermore, the velocity at which big data is generated, processed, and updated can make it hard to keep up with security monitoring and incident response.

Securing the Internet of Things

The Internet of Things (IoT) presents another set of cybersecurity challenges. As everyday objects from fridges to fitness trackers become connected to the internet, they offer more entry points for hackers. Many IoT devices lack robust built-in security features, making them vulnerable to attacks. The data they generate can be sensitive and personal, making breaches particularly invasive.

Given the distributed nature of IoT systems, traditional centralized security solutions may not be suitable. As such, securing the IoT requires novel approaches, such as edge computing security measures, advanced encryption techniques, and improved device authentication methods.

The Human Factor

While technological solutions form the backbone of cybersecurity, the human factor should not be overlooked. People are often the weakest link in the cybersecurity chain. Phishing attacks, which trick individuals into revealing sensitive information, remain one of the most common types of cyber threats.

Enhancing cybersecurity awareness and practices among all internet users is therefore vital. This includes using strong, unique passwords, being wary of suspicious emails or websites, and keeping software and devices updated. Organizations can also instill a culture of cybersecurity, where employees are educated on best practices and encouraged to report potential threats.

The Future of Cybersecurity

Looking ahead, the future of cybersecurity lies in continuously staying ahead of cyber threats. As hackers become more sophisticated, so too must our defenses. Artificial intelligence and machine learning can play a significant role in this, helping to identify and respond to threats more rapidly and accurately. For example, machine learning algorithms can analyze patterns of network traffic to detect anomalies that might indicate a cyberattack.

However, the use of AI in cybersecurity also raises ethical and privacy considerations. For instance, how can we ensure that AI security tools respect user privacy when they monitor network activities? Balancing security and privacy will be a critical challenge for the future of cybersecurity.

The issue of cybersecurity extends beyond the realm of technology professionals. It is a shared responsibility that involves governments, businesses, and individuals. Governments need to implement robust legal frameworks that penalize cybercrime, encourage cybersecurity best practices, and promote cooperation between countries.

Businesses must prioritize cybersecurity in their operations, investing in advanced security technologies and fostering a security-aware culture. Individuals must take steps to protect their own online activities, such as using secure passwords, regularly updating their devices, and being vigilant against suspicious online activities.

Moreover, it's crucial to foster a culture of transparency and collaboration in cybersecurity. The sharing of threat intelligence among organizations can enhance collective defenses, making it harder for cybercriminals to succeed. However, this needs to be done in a manner that respects privacy and trust. There is also a pressing need to address the cybersecurity skills gap, through education and training initiatives that prepare more people for careers in cybersecurity.

As we forge ahead in this data-rich landscape, cybersecurity will remain a persistent and evolving challenge. However, by understanding the threats, implementing robust defenses, and working together, we can safeguard the promise of big data and the internet of things.

The ultimate goal is to create a cyber landscape where security and innovation go hand in hand, enabling the full potential of the sentient web while protecting against its potential perils.

In the grand scheme of things, cybersecurity in the era of big data and the internet of things is not just about protecting bits and bytes, but about safeguarding our way of life in the digital age. From our personal privacy to our economic stability, to our national security, the stakes could not be higher. And as we embark on this digital journey, our ability to navigate the challenges of cybersecurity will be a crucial determinant of how the story of the sentient web unfolds.

This digital revolution holds the promise of unprecedented opportunities, but it also presents significant challenges. Cybersecurity, a concept almost unheard of a few decades ago, is now at the forefront of our digital lives. And while the threats are real and ever-evolving, so too is our ability to innovate and adapt. In this high-stakes game of cat and mouse, we are not helpless.

We have the knowledge, the tools, and the will to fight back. And as long as we keep the dialogue open, continue to learn, and refuse to be complacent, we can look forward to a future where technology serves us, rather than the other way around.

Chapter 4: The Ethical Dilemmas of a Sentient Web

The Intersection of Artificial Intelligence and Ethics

In a world where artificial intelligence is becoming increasingly prominent, we find ourselves not just in a digital revolution but at the precipice of an ethical transformation. As AI systems pervade various aspects of our lives, from smart home gadgets to advanced medical diagnostics, to autonomous vehicles, it brings forth questions that go beyond technical implementation and breach into the realm of ethics. The ethical implications of AI can't be understated; these technologies hold the power to reshape society, for better or worse, depending on how we handle them.

The first major ethical consideration in AI involves the concept of transparency. The so-called 'black box' problem is a prominent issue in AI. This problem refers to AI systems making decisions without humans being able to understand how these decisions were arrived at. For example, a machine learning algorithm may reject a loan application, but we can't comprehend why that decision was made. This lack of transparency not only creates trust issues, but it also raises legal and ethical concerns, particularly when AI is used in areas such as healthcare, finance, or judicial systems.

Another significant ethical quandary revolves around privacy. In the age of big data, privacy is more than just a personal matter; it's a fundamental human right. As AI systems require enormous amounts of data to function effectively, the risk to individual privacy intensifies. We've seen this debate play out with personal digital assistants, social media platforms, and targeted online ads, among others. Balancing the benefits of personalization with privacy protection is a major challenge in this data-driven era.

Bias in AI systems is also a crucial ethical concern. AI systems are trained on data collected from the real world, which can often contain human biases. These biases can become ingrained in the AI system, leading to unfair outcomes. For instance, an AI used in hiring may discriminate against certain demographics if the training data reflected such biases. Confronting these biases and ensuring fairness in AI outcomes is essential.

Furthermore, the impact of AI on employment is another ethical issue. Automation threatens to replace certain job categories, particularly those involving repetitive tasks. While it could also create new jobs, the transition period may be painful for many, with potential social and economic disruption. The ethics of this employment transformation require serious debate and thoughtful policy responses.

Finally, the concept of sentient AI and machine agency stirs deep philosophical and ethical questions. As we move towards creating more sophisticated AI systems capable of autonomous decision-making, at what point do we attribute some form of 'sentience' or 'rights' to these machines? What happens if AI surpasses human intelligence, a scenario known as the singularity? The implications are profound and merit thorough exploration.

Addressing these ethical dilemmas is not a task for the future; it's a responsibility that we must undertake now. Ethics should be a primary consideration during the design and implementation of AI systems, not an afterthought. It's crucial to establish strong ethical guidelines and regulatory frameworks to govern the use of AI. Policymakers, technologists, ethicists, and society at large need to engage in an ongoing dialogue to navigate these ethical challenges effectively.

Moreover, fostering ethical literacy in AI and technology should be a key part of education. From early education to professional training, individuals should be equipped with the knowledge to understand and debate these complex issues. Promoting a culture of ethical awareness and responsibility in technology is fundamental to ensuring that the sentient web benefits all of humanity.

In the subsequent sections of this chapter, we will delve deeper into these ethical dilemmas, exploring each issue in detail and discussing potential strategies to address them. This exploration will not provide all the answers, but it aims to spur thought, inspire conversation, and guide us as we embark on a journey through uncharted territory, balancing on the knife-edge of rapid technological advancements and their ethical ramifications.

The 'black box' problem in AI, for instance, is not an insurmountable challenge. Techniques such as Explainable AI (XAI) are emerging to address this issue, where the focus is on creating AI systems that provide insights into their internal workings. These efforts aim to make AI decisions transparent, comprehensible, and thus, more trustworthy. However, they also call for a recalibration of our understanding of accountability in an era increasingly defined by machine agency.

Equally, tackling the issue of privacy in the age of big data is not a lost cause. The introduction of privacy-preserving technologies such as differential privacy and federated learning offers promising avenues. These techniques aim to provide the benefits of data analysis while protecting individual privacy. However, their effective implementation requires revising our existing data governance frameworks and possibly redefining what we consider as 'privacy' in the digital age.

When it comes to bias in AI systems, awareness and proactive measures are key. Bias mitigation techniques are being developed to reduce the impact of unfair biases in AI models. Algorithmic audits can be conducted to test AI systems for bias and fairness. However, it's important to remember that technology is not a panacea; addressing societal biases that seep into our data is a larger, collective responsibility.

As for the impact of AI on jobs, a blend of policies and strategies could be helpful. This includes initiatives for reskilling and upskilling workers, promoting lifelong learning, and implementing social safety nets for those affected by automation. While there's no one-size-fits-all solution, the focus should be on creating an inclusive, sustainable, and human-centric future of work.

Finally, navigating the philosophical and ethical maze around machine sentience is perhaps the most complex and abstract of all these dilemmas. The question of machine rights is closely linked to how we define concepts such as consciousness, self-awareness, and suffering, which are profoundly complex and continue to baffle even our brightest minds. This debate stretches the boundaries of our ethical and philosophical discourse, signaling the dawn of a new era of 'machine ethics'.

In the end, navigating the ethical dilemmas of a sentient web is a collective and iterative process. As the philosopher Kwame Anthony Appiah once said, "Ethics is not a spectator sport." It requires active participation from all of us – policymakers, technologists, ethicists, and everyday citizens. The future of the sentient web will be determined not just by technological advancements but by our collective ethical compass.

As we move deeper into this fascinating journey, we have the power to shape the sentient web's trajectory in a way that aligns with our most cherished human values. The challenges are numerous, but so are the opportunities. It's an endeavor that calls not just for scientific prowess, but also for philosophical wisdom, ethical insight, and, above all, a shared commitment to a future that embodies the best of human and machine agency.

Digital Ethics: Guiding Principles for a New Era

As we navigate the uncharted territory of the sentient web, ethics isn't just a footnote; it is a central theme that interweaves the entire narrative. Digital ethics, in particular, helps to set the moral compass for this journey, allowing us to align technological advancements with human values. The urgent need for a solid ethical framework arises from the fact that digital technologies, with their capacity to process vast amounts of data and make autonomous decisions, have deeply permeated our lives, influencing our choices, behaviors, and relationships.

The first step towards a solid ethical foundation is acknowledging the shared human responsibility to shape digital technologies. Too often, ethics is seen as the sole responsibility of a dedicated 'ethics committee' or a few philosophers, when in reality, every designer, developer, user, or policymaker plays a role in shaping the ethical trajectory of digital technologies. As the saying goes, 'ethics is a team sport'.

Inclusivity, a cornerstone of any ethical framework, gains paramount importance in the digital context. The digital world should be a place where everyone, regardless of their age, gender, race, or socio-economic status, feels welcomed and empowered. Efforts towards digital inclusivity could involve making technologies accessible for differently-abled individuals, ensuring fair representation in data and AI systems, and bridging the digital divide that leaves many people disenfranchised in the age of the internet.

Transparency is another key ethical principle, especially with complex AI systems that often operate as 'black boxes'. Users should have a clear understanding of how their data is being used, and the logic behind the decisions made by AI systems that impact their lives. Beyond being a tool for fostering trust, transparency is a means of promoting accountability and responsibility in the digital space.

Finally, respect for user autonomy is a non-negotiable aspect of digital ethics. While AI systems can provide valuable recommendations or predictions, it is crucial to ensure that they do not unduly influence or manipulate user choices. Providing opt-out options, empowering users to control their data, and maintaining a human-in-the-loop for significant decisions are strategies to respect and uphold user autonomy.

Internet Ethics: The Morality of the Online World

Moving onto the specifics of internet ethics, we delve into the moral landscape of the online world, an expansive universe that houses a myriad of interactions, transactions, and creations. The first point of discussion is the digital dualism that often shapes our perception of the online world. It's essential to recognize that the internet isn't a separate realm detached from 'real life'; the actions, decisions, and interactions in the online world have tangible impacts on individuals and society.

A key principle of internet ethics is fostering respectful interactions. With the cloak of anonymity, online spaces often become breeding grounds for hate speech, bullying, or harassment. Encouraging digital empathy, promoting community moderation, and creating effective reporting mechanisms are critical to maintaining the decorum of online spaces.

Protecting privacy in the online world is another pressing ethical issue. As data becomes the lifeblood of the internet, the issue of data consent, protection, and usage gains center stage. Here, the 'privacy by design' principle, which integrates privacy protections into the product design process itself, is an approach that aligns with the ethical requirements of the online world.

Intellectual property rights in the online world also warrant ethical consideration. As creations and ideas freely float in the online space, it's crucial to strike a balance between encouraging creativity and protecting the rights of creators.

Lastly, ensuring digital literacy is an ethical mandate in the age of the internet. As the internet becomes a vital part of education, work, and social life, ensuring that individuals have the skills to navigate the online world safely and effectively becomes paramount.

Both digital and internet ethics revolve around a common goal: ensuring that the digital transformation uplifts human society rather than posing threats to our values or our ways of life. This involves a collaborative, ongoing effort to create technologies and policies that reflect our ethical commitments, even as these commitments continue to evolve and deepen in the light of new technological capabilities.

The Role of Governance in Digital Ethics

Governance structures, including laws, regulations, and norms, play a crucial role in guiding ethical behavior in the digital and online world. However, the transnational nature of the internet, coupled with the rapid pace of technological innovation, poses significant challenges to effective governance. Striking a balance between regulation and innovation is a delicate act, one that requires foresight, collaboration, and flexibility.

For example, data protection laws, such as the General Data Protection Regulation (GDPR) in the European

Union, have become vital tools in safeguarding user privacy. These laws stipulate the rights of individuals over their data and impose obligations on organizations that collect, process, and store this data. However, these laws also need to evolve with technological advancements, such as the emergence of AI and machine learning technologies, which challenge traditional notions of data privacy and consent.

Self-regulation by technology companies is another form of governance that can play a role in upholding digital ethics. Tech companies can build ethics into their design and decision-making processes, adopt privacy-enhancing technologies, and foster a culture of ethical sensitivity among their workforce. However, the effectiveness of self-regulation is often limited by conflicts of interest, and hence, needs to be supplemented by external oversight and regulation.

The ethics of a sentient web is a broad, multifaceted domain that encompasses issues of privacy, transparency, accountability, respect, inclusivity, and more. As we venture further into the digital age, these ethical considerations will only become more complex and urgent. It's up to us – the creators, users, and governors of technology – to navigate these challenges and steer our digital future towards a path that aligns with our shared human values. The discussions in this chapter provide a starting point for this critical journey.

Addressing the Unintended Consequences of Automation

As we continue to entrust machines with more tasks, our society finds itself in the throes of an automation revolution. Every revolution brings change, and while the benefits are often well-celebrated, it's equally essential to give due attention to the potential challenges and unintended consequences. As we move forward on this unprecedented path, it becomes imperative to not only appreciate the advantages automation brings but also understand, anticipate, and mitigate its possible unintended consequences.

To begin with, let's talk about what automation brings to the table. The primary allure of automation is its ability to perform repetitive tasks with unprecedented speed, precision, and consistency. Automated systems don't experience fatigue, they don't need breaks, and their performance doesn't waver under stressful conditions. This enables organizations to increase productivity, improve quality, and enhance reliability. Automation also presents the potential for increased safety by taking humans out of the equation in hazardous environments or tasks.

However, the very characteristics that make automation so attractive can also give rise to a series of unintended consequences that are critical to consider.

Job Displacement and Skills Mismatch

Perhaps the most commonly discussed unintended consequence of automation is job displacement. The fear that robots and algorithms might take away jobs is not unfounded. It's an economic reality that as tasks become automated, the demand for human labor to perform those tasks diminishes. This can lead to job loss in sectors where automation is heavily implemented.

But it's not just about jobs disappearing; it's also about the changing nature of the jobs that remain. Automation tends to replace tasks within jobs rather than entire occupations. This means that the skill requirements for many jobs are changing. As machines take over routine and repetitive tasks, there's a growing demand for skills that machines currently lack, such as creativity, critical thinking, emotional intelligence, and complex problem-solving. Consequently, we may face a skills mismatch, where the workforce doesn't have the skills that the job market demands.

Addressing this challenge requires foresight, planning, and collective action. Governments, businesses, and educational institutions need to collaborate to identify the skills of the future and revise curricula to align with these needs. Lifelong learning and re-skilling initiatives need to be championed to help the existing workforce adapt to the changing job landscape.

Inequality

The effects of automation aren't evenly distributed across society. There are winners and losers. This can exacerbate socioeconomic inequalities. For instance, jobs involving routine tasks are more susceptible to automation and are often held by individuals in lower income brackets. On the other hand, those with the resources and skills to develop, deploy, or work alongside automated systems stand to benefit the most.

Furthermore, as companies deploy automation technologies to save costs, the economic gains often flow to business owners and shareholders, potentially widening the wealth gap.

Policies that promote equitable access to the benefits of automation are crucial. This could include progressive taxation, universal basic income, or other forms of wealth redistribution. The aim should be to ensure that the prosperity generated by automation is widely shared rather than concentrated in the hands of a few.

Dependence and Vulnerability

As we grow more reliant on automated systems, we also become more vulnerable to their failure or misuse. Faulty algorithms can make poor decisions with far-reaching impacts. Automated systems can also be targets of cyberattacks, leading to disastrous consequences, especially in critical infrastructure such as power grids or healthcare systems.

Moreover, over-reliance on automation can lead to skill degradation in humans, as they get out of practice doing tasks that machines have taken over. This can pose serious problems when humans need to take over in cases of machine failure.

To mitigate these risks, we need robust design practices, thorough testing of automated systems, and cybersecurity measures. It's also essential to maintain a human-in-the-loop approach where appropriate, ensuring that humans stay involved and competent in the automated tasks.

Ethical and Legal Dilemmas

Automation can blur the lines of responsibility and pose ethical and legal challenges. For instance, if an autonomous vehicle is involved in an accident, who is to blame? The manufacturer of the vehicle, the developer of the AI, or the owner of the car? And if an algorithm used in hiring practices discriminates against certain groups, who is responsible?

To navigate these issues, we need to develop clear legal frameworks that outline responsibilities and liabilities in the context of automation. The development and deployment of automated systems should also be guided by ethical principles that prioritize fairness, transparency, and respect for human rights.

Implications for Mental Health and Well-being

The increasing automation of tasks can also have profound impacts on our mental health and well-being. It can lead to increased stress and anxiety, especially among those whose jobs are threatened by automation. Work provides not just income, but often a sense of identity and purpose. Therefore, the prospect of automation can evoke feelings of insecurity and existential dread.

Moreover, as more of our social interactions move online, mediated by algorithms, we risk feeling isolated and disconnected. Algorithmic feeds can lead to echo chambers, exacerbating polarization and misinformation. To address these concerns, mental health and well-being need to be central considerations in how we design and deploy automation technologies. Moreover, a greater emphasis on social security nets can also play a role in alleviating some of the psychological stress associated with the uncertainties of automation.

As we continue to steer our society towards increased automation, it's vital to navigate the transition with care, foresight, and a commitment to shared prosperity. Automation, when thoughtfully managed and implemented, can bring numerous benefits. However, it's also fraught with potential pitfalls and unintended consequences that need to be thoughtfully addressed. A balanced approach, coupled with proactive policies and practices, can ensure we harness the benefits of automation while minimizing its downsides. By doing so, we can move towards a future where humans and machines co-exist and thrive in a mutually beneficial, balanced ecosystem.

Rethinking Human Rights in the AI Age

The evolution of AI and its omnipresence in our daily lives has prompted a profound reevaluation of human rights in the context of the digital era. Just as the advent of industrialization necessitated labor laws and the rise of the internet led to the creation of data privacy regulations, so too does the emergence of AI call for a critical reassessment of our current human rights framework.

At the heart of this issue is the recognition that AI technologies have the potential to both empower and disenfranchise. They can provide unprecedented opportunities, facilitating global connectivity, democratizing information, aiding medical diagnosis, and more. Yet, they also pose significant threats to privacy, equality, freedom of expression, and other fundamental rights.

From Privacy to Data Dignity

Privacy rights have long been a cornerstone of human rights, and the transition into the AI era has amplified the importance of this principle. With AI systems built on vast amounts of personal data, concerns about privacy intrusions have risen exponentially. Surveillance technologies, facial recognition systems, and data mining practices can invade individual privacy, tracking movements, predicting behaviors, and infringing on personal spaces.

To address this, we must transition from merely a focus on privacy to a broader concept of 'data dignity.' This term emphasizes the intrinsic value and personal investment in the data we generate. It suggests that individuals should have control over their data, and that they should be compensated fairly if their data is used. By promoting data dignity, we can ensure a more equitable data economy where individuals are respected as crucial contributors rather than mere data sources.

Promoting Equality in the Age of AI

AI technologies, particularly machine learning algorithms, can inadvertently perpetuate and amplify existing biases, leading to discrimination in critical areas such as employment, education, and criminal justice. These biases can be traced back to the data used to train these algorithms, which often reflect the prejudices present in society.

The challenge here is to ensure that AI systems promote rather than undermine equality. To achieve this, it's essential to develop rigorous algorithmic auditing practices to identify and mitigate biases. There should also be diverse representation in AI development teams to ensure a multiplicity of perspectives in the creation of these systems.

Moreover, transparency around AI decision-making processes is crucial. The so-called 'black box' nature of some AI systems, where inputs and outputs are known but the internal workings are not, is a significant barrier to this transparency. Progress must be made towards explainable AI, where decisions made by AI systems can be understood by human users.

Freedom of Expression and Information

The rise of AI has implications for freedom of expression and access to information. On the one hand, AI technologies can facilitate access to information, making it easier to sort through vast amounts of data and connect people with relevant content. On the other hand, AI algorithms can also create 'filter bubbles' or 'echo chambers,' where people are exposed primarily to viewpoints that align with their own, leading to polarization and misinformation.

Here, the challenge is to balance the beneficial personalization of content with the need for a diverse and balanced information environment. This requires careful algorithm design and regulation, along with increased media literacy among users to navigate the digital information landscape effectively.

Redefining Human Rights for the AI Age

To conclude, the AI age necessitates a rethinking of human rights. The existing human rights framework provides a solid foundation, but it needs to be expanded and adapted to address the unique challenges and opportunities posed by AI technologies.

This involves broadening our understanding of existing rights, such as privacy, and possibly articulating new rights, such as the right to explanation for decisions made by AI. It also involves developing new mechanisms for upholding these rights, such as algorithmic audits and impact assessments.

Ultimately, rethinking human rights in the AI age means grappling with complex ethical, legal, and technical issues. But it also represents an opportunity. It's a chance to shape the development of AI technologies in ways that respect human dignity, promote equality, and support a fair and open society.

We're entering a time of dynamic interaction between technology and human rights, one that requires the active involvement of all stakeholders – from technologists, policymakers, and ethicists to the wider public. The AI future is not a foregone conclusion; it's one that we all have a hand in shaping.

The Right to Autonomy and the AI Landscape

The concept of personal autonomy – the capacity to be the author of one's life – is another right that needs reevaluation in the context of AI. AI systems can make predictions, suggestions, and decisions that impact our lives profoundly, sometimes without our explicit consent.

For instance, consider an AI system that uses personal data to predict health risks and suggest lifestyle modifications. While this could be beneficial, it could also be seen as an intrusion into personal autonomy, especially if the individual is not fully informed or if the AI system's advice is followed without critical scrutiny.

Recognizing and upholding the right to autonomy in the age of AI involves ensuring that individuals have control over when and how AI technologies are used in their lives. It means providing clear and comprehensive information about how AI systems operate and the implications of their use. It also involves ensuring that individuals have the ability to contest decisions made by AI and to opt out of certain uses of AI if they so choose.

Artificial Intelligence and Access to Opportunities

AI's transformative potential could either bridge or widen the gap in access to opportunities. AI technologies can improve access to education, healthcare, and employment, enabling personalized learning, telemedicine, and efficient job matching. However, without careful oversight, they could also entrench existing inequalities.

Consider, for example, the use of AI in hiring. AI can streamline the recruitment process, identifying potential candidates from a vast pool of applicants. However, if the algorithm unintentionally incorporates biases, it may systematically favor certain groups over others, leading to discrimination.

Ensuring equitable access to opportunities in the AI era requires a two-pronged approach. On the one hand, it involves harnessing AI's potential to break down barriers and create opportunities. On the other hand, it necessitates robust measures to prevent and redress AI-enabled discrimination.

The Urgency of Rethinking Human Rights

The rise of AI has created an urgent need for a thorough rethinking of human rights. The AI landscape, with its unique potential and challenges, requires a recalibration of traditional human rights concepts and possibly the articulation of new rights altogether.

This is a challenging endeavor, but it is not insurmountable. The goal is clear: to ensure that as AI technologies become an integral part of our world, they are harnessed in ways that respect, protect, and fulfill human rights. The path towards achieving this goal will involve continued dialogue, collaborative problem-solving, and innovative thinking across sectors and disciplines. As we navigate this path, we are not merely responding to the rise of AI - we are shaping the future of human rights in the digital age.

The Role of Government, Business, and Civil Society in AI Ethics

In the rapidly evolving digital landscape, the ethical challenges posed by AI aren't just technological issues—they're societal ones. Addressing these challenges requires a concerted, multi-stakeholder effort. Government, business, and civil society each have vital roles to play, and the success of AI ethics depends on their effective collaboration.

The Role of Government: Regulation and Policy-Making

In the world of AI, governments hold a dual role as regulators and consumers of technology. As regulators, they create the policy framework within which AI operates. These frameworks include laws, regulations, and guidelines that set the rules of the game—rules that protect the public interest while encouraging innovation.

Regulation in the AI field needs to be flexible enough to adapt to the rapid pace of technological change. This may mean implementing "soft law" approaches, such as guidelines and standards, that can evolve more rapidly than traditional legislation. It also means ensuring that regulators have the resources and expertise necessary to oversee the complex, dynamic field of AI.

As consumers of AI technologies, governments can help shape the market by prioritizing ethical considerations in their procurement decisions. By doing so, they can encourage the development of AI technologies that respect privacy, fairness, transparency, and accountability.

The Role of Business: Responsible Innovation and Corporate Accountability

Businesses are at the frontlines of AI development and deployment. Their role in AI ethics is twofold: responsible innovation and corporate accountability.

Responsible innovation involves integrating ethical considerations into the AI design and development process. This means adopting a "human-in-the-loop" approach that ensures AI technologies respect human values and norms. It also means taking a proactive stance towards potential risks, by implementing robust risk management practices and conducting impact assessments.

Corporate accountability involves ensuring that businesses are held responsible for the ethical implications of their AI technologies. This may mean implementing auditing mechanisms that allow for the transparent and independent review of AI systems. It also means creating channels for redress when AI systems harm individuals or communities.

The Role of Civil Society: Advocacy, Education, and Oversight

Civil society groups, including non-governmental organizations, academic institutions, and grassroots movements, play a crucial role in AI ethics.

As advocates, civil society groups can raise public awareness about the ethical implications of AI and push for policy changes. They can amplify the voices of those most likely to be affected by AI technologies, ensuring that their interests are considered in policy debates.

As educators, civil society groups can help improve public understanding of AI. This includes not only raising awareness about potential risks but also helping people understand how they can use AI technologies to empower themselves and their communities.

As overseers, civil society groups can help hold businesses and governments accountable. They can scrutinize the activities of these actors, highlight ethical breaches, and push for corrective action.

Conclusion: Synergy for Ethical AI

The ethical challenges posed by AI are complex and multifaceted, and no single actor can address them alone. Governments, businesses, and civil society each bring unique capabilities and perspectives to the table. By working together, they can develop comprehensive, effective responses to these challenges.

Building ethical AI isn't just about avoiding harm—it's about realizing the positive potential of AI. It's about creating AI technologies that respect our values, support social equity, and empower individuals and communities. This is an ambitious goal, but with the concerted efforts of governments, businesses, and civil society, it's a goal within our reach.

Chapter 5: The Digital Rights and Responsibilities

Digital Rights: Freedom and Protection in the Cyberspace

We stand on the brink of a digital revolution that is reshaping the very fabric of our societies. This transition is not just about technology; it's about the rights and responsibilities that underpin our digital interactions. Let's unpack the concept of digital rights and explore how they relate to freedom and protection in cyberspace.

Digital rights, much like human rights, are the inherent rights individuals possess in the digital sphere. They form the bedrock of our online existence, affecting how we express ourselves, access information, and interact with others. These rights include freedom of expression, privacy, access to information, and protection from harm. But in the labyrinth of cyberspace, upholding these rights is not a straightforward task.

Freedom of Expression in Cyberspace

In the digital age, the right to freedom of expression extends far beyond spoken or written words. It includes the right to share ideas, opinions, and information through digital platforms, from social media to blogs and beyond. The internet, with its global reach, provides a powerful platform for people to voice their views, sparking dialogues that transcend national boundaries.

Yet, this digital freedom of expression is under threat. Censorship, surveillance, and online harassment can silence voices and stifle dissent. The challenge lies in striking a balance between enabling free expression and preventing harmful content, such as hate speech or disinformation.

Privacy: A Shield in the Digital World

Privacy in the digital world is about having control over your personal information—knowing what data is collected, how it's used, and who has access to it. But as the volume of online data skyrockets, so does the complexity of safeguarding privacy.

While AI and big data technologies offer immense benefits, they also create potential avenues for privacy breaches. Surveillance capitalism, data breaches, and invasive advertising are just a few examples of the privacy challenges we face in the digital age.

Access to Information: The Lifeline of the Digital Society

Access to information is a crucial digital right, serving as the lifeline of our digital society. It's not just about accessing the internet—it's about the ability to access reliable, relevant, and diverse information. But with information overload, algorithmic biases, and digital divides, this right is far from guaranteed for everyone.

Protection from Harm: Safeguarding Digital Citizens

In the digital realm, individuals have the right to be protected from harm. This includes protection from cybercrime, online harassment, and other forms of digital harm. It also includes the right to digital literacy—the knowledge and skills needed to navigate the digital world safely and effectively.

Digital Rights are Human Rights

Digital rights are not separate from human rights—they are an extension of them. As we continue to integrate digital technologies into every aspect of our lives, the importance of digital rights will only grow. Upholding these rights will require a collective effort from all stakeholders, from government and businesses to civil society and individuals. The future of our digital society depends on it.

As our society becomes increasingly digitized, the significance of our digital rights cannot be overstated. They form the basis of our digital citizenship and define how we should interact in this new landscape. As we navigate through the rapidly changing digital environment, it's crucial that these rights are not just defined but actively protected and promoted.

Enforcing digital rights requires robust legal frameworks, responsible business practices, and an informed and empowered citizenry. Governments should prioritize the creation and enforcement of laws that protect digital rights, from data protection legislation to laws that ensure internet access for all. Businesses, especially those in the technology sector, should commit to ethical data practices, ensuring that they respect their users' rights to privacy and freedom of expression.

At the individual level, digital literacy is key. We must equip people with the skills and knowledge to understand their digital rights and to navigate the online world safely and effectively. Civil society, including educational institutions, NGOs, and media, has a critical role to play here, providing resources and platforms to foster digital literacy and awareness.

Moreover, it's important to remember that the digital world does not exist in isolation—it's intertwined with our offline world. Therefore, digital rights and offline human rights must be treated with equal importance and protection.

In the end, the digital revolution is not just about technology; it's about people. It's about how we interact, communicate, work, and live in the digital age. By upholding digital rights, we ensure that this revolution leads to a digital society that is not only technologically advanced but also fair, inclusive, and human-centered.

The discourse around digital rights is complex, evolving, and crucially important. It requires constant reflection, debate, and adjustments as technology continues to advance at a breakneck pace. As we stand on the threshold of the era of the Sentient Web, we must keep this dialogue alive, reminding ourselves that at the core of every technological advancement, every piece of code, and every byte of data, are humans with inherent rights that must be respected and protected. Our shared digital future depends on it.

Digital Citizenship: Responsibilities in a Digital Society

While it's essential to understand our digital rights, it's equally crucial to recognize our responsibilities as digital citizens in the connected world. As the old adage goes, "With great power comes great responsibility," and the power afforded to us by the digital world is monumental. It's not enough just to know our rights in this brave new world; we must also comprehend our duties and obligations, to ourselves, to others, and to the digital society in which we're immersed.

Being a responsible digital citizen can be seen as an extension of our traditional societal roles. It's about practicing ethics, displaying respect for others, and fostering a safe and inclusive online environment. Just as we have societal norms for behavior in the physical world, so too do we need norms for the digital world. However, the digital domain, with its global reach, anonymity, and potential for rapid dissemination of information, brings with it unique challenges that call for unique responsibilities.

One of the primary responsibilities we have as digital citizens is the duty of respect. Just as we're expected to treat others with kindness and understanding in person, we should do the same online. We must respect the rights of others to have and express differing opinions, recognizing that a diversity of perspectives enriches our digital society. But respect goes beyond accepting differing viewpoints. It also encompasses respect for privacy—both our own and that of others.

Respecting privacy online can be a tricky issue. With the proliferation of social media and online platforms, our lives are becoming increasingly public. It's often tempting to share every aspect of our lives online, and while there's nothing inherently wrong with sharing, it's essential to consider the potential implications for both ourselves and others. We need to be mindful of the information we disclose about ourselves and respect the privacy of others by not sharing their personal information without consent. This caution extends to businesses as well, which have a responsibility to protect the data of their users.

The second key responsibility is the duty of honesty. In an age where misinformation can spread quickly and have serious consequences, the integrity of the information we share is paramount. We should always strive to share accurate information, to verify the sources of the news we share, and to correct any inaccuracies when they occur. Businesses, in turn, have a responsibility to be transparent with their customers and stakeholders, providing accurate and complete information about their products, services, and data practices.

Another responsibility in the digital society is the duty to keep ourselves and others safe. The online world can be a dangerous place, with threats ranging from cyberbullying to identity theft. We must take steps to protect ourselves, such as using strong passwords, updating our software, and being cautious about the information we share. We should also be aware of the risks to others, particularly vulnerable groups like children and the elderly, and take steps to protect them.

Our duty extends to being responsible consumers of technology. With the increasing concern about the environmental impact of technology, it's crucial to consider the life cycle of our devices—from production to disposal—and to take steps to minimize our digital carbon footprint. This might mean choosing devices that are energy-efficient, recycling our old devices responsibly, or even reconsidering whether we need to upgrade to the latest device at all.

Finally, digital citizens have a responsibility to contribute positively to the online community. The Internet is an incredible platform for creativity, collaboration, and innovation, and we should strive to use it to its full potential. This might involve contributing to online discussions, sharing our knowledge and skills, or using digital platforms to promote social good.

The responsibilities of digital citizenship are not to be taken lightly. As we become more deeply intertwined with the digital world, these responsibilities become more critical to maintaining a safe, respectful, and vibrant online society. Understanding and embracing these responsibilities is the cornerstone of a successful and ethical digital existence.

Of course, being responsible online also requires continuous learning. The digital world is constantly evolving, and with it, so are the challenges and threats we face. The techniques that we use today to keep our information secure, for example, might not be effective tomorrow. New ethical dilemmas could arise as technology advances. Staying informed about the latest trends, risks, and best practices in digital safety and ethics is a continuous responsibility for all digital citizens.

While individuals carry a significant part of the responsibility, it doesn't rest solely on their shoulders. Corporations, the creators and maintainers of much of the digital realm, also have a duty. They must ensure their platforms are safe and respect users' rights, and they must take a proactive stance against harmful behaviors like cyberbullying or misinformation. They must also consider the societal and environmental impacts of their products and services and strive for transparency in their practices.

Governments also have a role to play. They must strike a delicate balance between protecting citizens' rights and safety and maintaining an open, free internet. Legislation, policy making, and enforcement in the areas of data protection, privacy, and cybersecurity are essential tasks for government bodies. They must also promote digital literacy and awareness as a vital part of modern education.

Furthermore, civil society organizations can provide a supportive role, advocating for digital rights, raising awareness of issues, and providing resources for digital education and assistance. These groups can often provide a valuable bridge between policy, business, and the public, ensuring that the voices of ordinary digital citizens are heard.

The responsibilities of digital citizenship are complex and multifaceted, but they are not insurmountable. With education, awareness, and a commitment to ethical behavior, we can all contribute to a digital society that is safe, respectful, and inclusive. A society that not only understands the challenges posed by the digital world, but also recognizes the incredible opportunities it presents.

Digital citizenship isn't just about being able to navigate the digital world. It's about doing so responsibly, ethically, and productively. It's about knowing how to protect and respect ourselves and others, and understanding how our actions in the digital world can have far-reaching consequences. Most importantly, it's about realizing that we all have a role to play in shaping the digital society of the future.

As we move further into the era of the sentient web, these responsibilities will only grow in importance. Each of us, from individuals to large corporations, will need to play our part in creating a digital world that respects rights and champions ethical behavior. The path ahead isn't without its challenges, but if we approach it with understanding, respect, and a sense of duty, we can create a digital society that benefits us all.

Case Study: The Battle for Internet Governance

The power of the Internet as a tool for connection, communication, and collaboration is beyond dispute. It has transformed the way we live, work, learn, and interact. However, with this incredible power comes a significant challenge - how should the Internet be governed? Who gets to make the rules and set the standards? Who holds the keys to this digital kingdom? The battle for Internet governance is a complex, multifaceted issue that impacts every user of the Internet, and therefore, nearly every person on the planet.

A Melting Pot of Stakeholders

The first challenge in the battle for Internet governance is that the Internet is a truly global entity, and it crosses geographical and jurisdictional boundaries. This makes it a melting pot of various stakeholders, each with their own interests, agendas, and perspectives. These stakeholders include governments, businesses, civil society groups, academia, the technical community, and of course, individual users.

Each of these groups have different views on how the Internet should be governed. Governments often seek to maintain control over information and communication within their borders, which can lead to issues such as censorship or the suppression of dissent. Businesses, particularly large technology companies, have significant influence due to their role in developing and maintaining Internet infrastructure and platforms. Civil society groups and individual users generally advocate for an open, free Internet where information flows freely and digital rights are protected.

Decentralization vs. Centralization

A key battle in Internet governance is the struggle between decentralization and centralization. The Internet was originally designed to be decentralized, with no single point of control. This design philosophy has been crucial in enabling the Internet's rapid growth and its ability to withstand various types of disruption.

However, the Internet today is significantly more centralized than its original design. A small number of technology companies control large portions of the

Internet's infrastructure and services. Governments also exert control through regulations and, in some cases, direct control over Internet infrastructure within their borders.

This trend towards centralization has raised concerns about issues such as censorship, privacy, and the concentration of power. However, decentralization also presents challenges. It can make it harder to tackle issues such as cybercrime, misinformation, and hate speech, which require a coordinated response.

Governance Models

There are several models of Internet governance that have been proposed and implemented to varying degrees. These models often represent a compromise between the different interests of stakeholders.

The multistakeholder model is one approach that has gained significant traction. It involves the participation of all stakeholder groups in decision-making processes. The Internet Corporation for Assigned Names and Numbers (ICANN), which oversees the domain name system, operates on a multistakeholder model. This model is favored by many as it offers a democratic, inclusive approach to Internet governance.

Another model is the multilateral model, which involves governments as the main decision-makers. This model is often favored by countries that seek greater control over the Internet within their borders.

Yet, no model is without its critics. The multistakeholder model, while democratic, can be slow and inefficient. It can also be influenced by those with the most resources. The multilateral model, on the other hand, risks leading to a fragmented Internet, governed by a patchwork of national regulations.

The Future of Internet Governance

As the battle for Internet governance rages on, the future remains uncertain. What is clear, however, is that the decisions made today will have far-reaching impacts on the future of the Internet and our digital society. It's crucial that these decisions are made with care, and with the interests of all stakeholders in mind.

The Internet has become an essential part of our lives, a public good that should be accessible, safe, and beneficial for everyone. Therefore, its governance should embrace the same principles. It should prioritize the protection of user rights, ensuring that digital freedoms are not traded away in the pursuit of other objectives, such as security or economic growth.

Moreover, Internet governance should aim to reduce, not exacerbate, inequalities. The digital divide remains a significant issue, with many people around the world still lacking reliable access to the Internet. Governance structures should therefore seek to promote inclusivity and accessibility, ensuring that everyone can participate in the digital society.

Additionally, the governance of the Internet should be adaptable and flexible. The pace of technological change means that new challenges and opportunities are constantly emerging. Governance structures must be capable of responding to these changes in a timely and effective manner.

At the same time, the importance of transparency cannot be overstated. Decisions about the governance of the Internet should be made in an open and transparent manner, to maintain public trust and ensure accountability. Stakeholders must also engage in constructive dialogue and work towards consensus wherever possible.

Finally, the complexity and global nature of the Internet means that cooperation will be essential. No single stakeholder group can govern the Internet effectively on its own. Governments, businesses, civil society groups, and individuals must all work together to address the challenges and harness the opportunities of the digital age.

The battle for Internet governance is not just about technical details or administrative control. It's about who gets to shape the digital society of the future. It's about who gets to decide how our rights and freedoms are protected online. And ultimately, it's about how we can ensure that the Internet continues to be a force for good, enabling human progress and fostering a global community.

As we look to the future, it's clear that the battle for Internet governance will continue to be a critical part of the conversation on the future of the Internet and our digital society.

Chapter 6: The Regulatory Challenge: Balancing Freedom and Control

Internet Regulation: Need, Challenges, and Strategies

In an ever-connected world, the Internet has emerged as a thriving hub for innovation, communication, entertainment, and commerce. This incredibly complex and influential technology is no longer a luxury but a cornerstone of our modern society. With its permeating impact on all aspects of our lives, the discussion of regulating this digital behemoth has gained significant attention.

But when we talk about Internet regulation, we grapple with a plethora of dilemmas - how do we strike a balance between control and freedom? How do we ensure security while upholding privacy? How do we protect intellectual property without stifling innovation? The purpose of this chapter is to delve into the depths of these critical issues, reflect upon the need for Internet regulation, outline the inherent challenges, and suggest potential strategies.

The need for Internet regulation is primarily driven by three crucial factors: maintaining public order, safeguarding user rights, and fostering a healthy digital ecosystem. The rise in cybercrimes, online harassment, hate speech, misinformation, and terrorist activities on the web underscores the need for a sense of public order online. Without a degree of regulation, the Internet can become a lawless wild west where misconduct goes unpunished, creating a hostile environment for users.

Additionally, the protection of user rights such as privacy, freedom of speech, and non-discrimination necessitates a regulatory framework. Finally, fostering a healthy digital ecosystem that encourages competition, innovation, and economic growth is another compelling reason to consider Internet regulation.

However, Internet regulation is rife with challenges. Firstly, the global and borderless nature of the Internet defies the traditional regulatory approaches based on geographical jurisdictions. How can one country's regulations apply to a website hosted in another country but accessed globally? Secondly, the dynamic and rapidly evolving character of the Internet makes it hard for regulations to keep pace. Laws and regulations typically take years to develop and implement, but in the digital world, technologies and their applications can change significantly within months.

Another challenge stems from the conflict between competing interests and values. Consider the encryption debate. On one hand, encryption is a powerful tool for protecting user privacy and security. On the other, it can also be used by criminals to evade law enforcement. Striking a balance is a daunting task. Finally, there's the issue of enforcement. Even with regulations in place, monitoring compliance and enforcing these rules on the sprawling and intricate networks of the Internet is a Herculean task.

To overcome these challenges and to effectively regulate the Internet, a multifaceted strategy is required. Firstly, we need an international approach to Internet regulation. Collaborative international efforts could lead to the formation of a global regulatory framework. This would involve forging agreements, harmonizing policies, and establishing international standards. Organizations like the International Telecommunication Union (ITU) and Internet Corporation for Assigned Names and Numbers (ICANN) can play key roles in this endeavor.

Secondly, there should be a shift from reactive to proactive regulation. Instead of waiting for problems to arise and then creating regulations to address them, regulators should work closely with technologists, academics, and businesses to understand emerging technologies and anticipate potential issues. This way, we can create regulations that are ready for the future rather than always playing catch-up.

Furthermore, it's vital to create flexible and adaptable regulations. Given the speed at which technology evolves, rigid regulations can quickly become obsolete. Regulatory frameworks should therefore be designed to adapt to changing circumstances, perhaps by setting broad goals or principles rather than prescribing specific solutions.

Lastly, the strategy must involve the fostering of digital literacy. An informed user base can navigate the Internet more safely and make more responsible decisions online, reducing the need for regulation.

Internet regulation is a complex yet essential task. It is a delicate balancing act that requires us to maintain control over the potential harms while not stifling the immense benefits and freedoms that the Internet brings. This requires a comprehensive, thoughtful, and adaptive approach, one that is responsive to the fast-paced nature of the digital world and is built on international cooperation.

The technological realm is no longer a separate entity from the 'real' world. They have blurred and intermingled, making regulation more than just a question of maintaining order but also protecting our rights in this extended sphere of our lives. However, it is crucial to remember that regulation is not the end in itself but a means to create a safer, more equitable, and thriving digital environment.

The stakes in this endeavor are high. Done right, Internet regulation can help us tame the digital wild west without curbing its potential. Done wrong, it could lead to stifled innovation, infringed freedoms, and an oppressive digital environment. Hence, it is of paramount importance that we tread this path with a clear vision, cautious optimism, and an unwavering commitment to our digital rights and responsibilities.

It's a significant challenge, undoubtedly, but the results could shape the future of the Internet and, by extension, our society in the digital age. By understanding the need for Internet regulation, recognizing its inherent challenges, and strategizing effectively, we can move towards a digital world that harmonizes freedom and control, innovation and safety, and individual rights and collective welfare.

In the end, the success of this endeavor will be measured by our ability to create an Internet that is not just a network of machines, but a reflection of our shared values and hopes, an instrument of progress, and a testament to our capacity for collective action. The road ahead is undoubtedly complex and challenging, but with careful navigation, we can turn these challenges into milestones of our digital evolution.

Autonomous Systems and the Law: Regulatory Quandaries

Navigating the labyrinth of legal conundrums around autonomous systems is as intricate as the technology itself. From autonomous vehicles to AI-operated devices, autonomous systems are rapidly evolving, presenting a variety of challenges to our traditional legal frameworks. A regulatory gap has emerged, not only due to the rapid pace of technological advancements but also because of the novel questions they raise about accountability, privacy, safety, and ethics.

The first hurdle lies in defining what constitutes an 'autonomous system'. Generally, an autonomous system refers to any system capable of independent operation or decision-making. However, this broad definition blurs the line between various degrees of autonomy and the specific technologies involved. The wide-ranging nature of autonomous systems - from simple automated processes to highly complex AI algorithms - calls for a more nuanced classification system that can account for the different types and degrees of autonomy.

After the challenge of defining autonomy comes the question of legal personhood. As autonomous systems become more sophisticated, their actions become increasingly independent from human operators. This leads to a complex legal question: Who is responsible when something goes wrong? Traditional concepts of liability struggle to keep pace with the evolving autonomy in systems. This is because our current legal systems operate on the premise of human actors and human intent.

Take, for instance, the scenario of an autonomous vehicle involved in a traffic accident. Is the car's manufacturer liable because they produced the vehicle, or is the owner at fault, even if they had no active role in operating the vehicle at the time of the incident? Can the AI system be held responsible? While attributing legal personhood to an AI system may seem like a solution, it poses further complications, as legal personhood is traditionally associated with rights - a dimension we might not be ready to extend to AI systems.

On top of that, autonomous systems, by their very nature, are data-intensive. They rely on vast amounts of data to function effectively, often collecting, storing, and processing personal and sensitive information. This raises significant privacy concerns. The European Union's General Data Protection Regulation (GDPR) provides a certain degree of protection. Yet, the nuances of data handling in autonomous systems - such as continuous and dynamic data collection and the use of machine learning algorithms - present unique challenges to ensuring privacy.

Furthermore, the international nature of the digital landscape adds an extra layer of complexity. Autonomous systems operate in a global arena, transcending national jurisdictions. As a result, harmonizing laws across different countries becomes a vital but highly complex task. What's more, conflicts might arise between the regulations of a country where the system was developed and where it's operated.

In confronting these regulatory quandaries, we must strike a delicate balance. On one hand, we need to prevent harm and ensure accountability, privacy, and safety. On the other hand, overregulation risks stifling innovation and limiting the benefits of these technologies. A robust regulatory framework for autonomous systems, therefore, requires a collaborative, multi-disciplinary approach.

This begins with fostering dialogue between technologists, lawyers, policymakers, ethicists, and the public. Only through comprehensive and inclusive discussions can we hope to understand the full range of issues at hand and develop appropriate solutions.

Moreover, we need to rethink our approach to regulation. Traditional, rigid legislative processes may not be well suited to the dynamic nature of technological developments. Instead, a more flexible, iterative approach may be required – one that can adapt to new insights, technologies, and societal needs.

We must also consider a risk-based approach to regulation, focusing on the most high-stakes applications of autonomous systems. This means stricter regulations for autonomous systems used in, say, healthcare or transport, compared to those in less risk-sensitive areas.

Finally, international cooperation is crucial. Harmonizing laws across countries not only helps tackle jurisdictional issues but also promotes a global standard for safe and ethical use of autonomous systems. International treaties and agreements may play a pivotal role in this, setting the stage for a globally coordinated response.

As we inch closer to a future dominated by autonomous systems, it is crucial that we anticipate and address the myriad legal issues they raise. This isn't just about adapting our existing laws or creating new ones, but about fostering an ongoing dialogue about what kind of future we want to build.

While law typically lags behind technology, this gap poses significant risks when it comes to autonomous systems. A proactive approach to regulation is necessary to ensure that these technologies are developed and deployed responsibly.

In addition to laying down the rules, regulation is an important tool to build public trust in autonomous systems. Transparent laws, robust enforcement mechanisms, and clear liability rules can reassure the public that autonomous systems are safe, accountable, and respect their rights.

Moreover, regulation can guide the development of autonomous systems towards socially beneficial applications. By setting certain standards and expectations, laws can encourage developers to prioritize features that enhance safety, privacy, and fairness.

However, we must be mindful of the limitations of law as a tool to address the challenges posed by autonomous systems. Law can set the boundaries, but it cannot replace the need for ethical considerations in the design and use of these technologies.

The symbiosis of humans and machines envisaged in the sentient web needs to be underpinned by robust legal frameworks. But beyond that, it should be guided by our collective commitment to uphold human values and rights in the digital age.

As the saying goes, the devil is in the detail, and no truer is it than in our collective quest to establish a regulatory environment conducive to innovation and protective of our fundamental rights.

The digital transformation we are experiencing today is profound, exciting, and fraught with complexities. The realm of autonomous systems is no exception. But with proactive and collaborative efforts, we can ensure that these technologies evolve in a manner that aligns with our societal values, strengthens human agency, and nurtures the digital ecosystem we all inhabit.

As we venture further into the era of the sentient web, it is our shared responsibility to ensure that this digital frontier is governed by laws that are just, fair, and equitable. After all, the future of the sentient web is a reflection of our collective will.

Future of Internet Regulation: Predictions and Proposals

Gazing into the crystal ball of internet regulation, we find a kaleidoscope of challenges, opportunities, and transformative potential. In an era where the digital and physical realms are intricately woven together, our regulatory systems must evolve to maintain the balance between encouraging innovation and protecting the public interest. This section will offer some predictions about the future of internet regulation and put forward proposals to navigate this dynamic landscape.

A prominent trend we are likely to witness is the increase in global regulatory cooperation. The cross-border nature of the internet, coupled with the exponential growth of technologies like AI and IoT, necessitates a harmonized global regulatory approach. International treaties and cross-border enforcement alliances are likely to gain momentum, paving the way for a more cohesive and cooperative regulatory landscape. Moreover, standard-setting bodies and multinational organizations will play a pivotal role in shaping these international norms and guidelines.

However, achieving global regulatory cooperation is no easy task. National interests, economic disparities, and political ideologies often stand in the way. Therefore, fostering diplomatic dialogue and mutual understanding should be integral to this process. It is not about imposing a one-size-fits-all model, but rather, finding common ground that respects cultural diversity, protects human rights, and promotes digital equity.

As data continues to fuel the digital economy, regulations governing data privacy and protection are expected to become more stringent. Inspired by the GDPR, more countries are likely to enact comprehensive data protection laws. These laws will likely place greater emphasis on user consent, data minimization, and the right to be forgotten. Besides, as techniques like differential privacy gain traction, such practices could become regulatory requirements in the future.

The rise of decentralized technologies like blockchain also poses intriguing regulatory challenges. As these technologies disrupt traditional models of governance, regulators will be compelled to explore new paradigms. Rather than trying to fit these technologies into existing legal frameworks, we might see the emergence of 'regulatory sandboxes' – controlled environments where new technologies can be tested and regulatory strategies can be experimented with.

Regulatory innovation will likely become a key theme in the coming years. This includes adopting agile regulatory frameworks that can adapt to the fast-paced nature of technological change. It also involves experimenting with regulatory technologies (RegTech) that use AI and other technologies to enhance regulatory compliance and enforcement.

Looking ahead, the tech industry could face greater scrutiny and regulation. Anti-trust laws may be updated to prevent digital monopolies, while new laws may emerge to address issues like algorithmic bias, content moderation, and digital misinformation.

Turning to proposals, there are a few strategic directions that policymakers, industry, and civil society should consider. Firstly, fostering multi-stakeholder participation in internet regulation is essential. This includes engaging tech companies, civil society, academia, and users in the regulatory process. Such an inclusive approach ensures diverse perspectives are considered, fostering regulations that are balanced, informed, and fair.

Secondly, regulatory capacity building should be a priority. This involves educating policymakers about emerging technologies, and equipping them with the skills to design effective regulatory strategies. This also extends to the judiciary, who play a crucial role in interpreting and applying these laws.

Thirdly, the principles of transparency, accountability, and fairness should underpin internet regulation. Transparent laws and practices help build public trust, while strong accountability mechanisms ensure that these laws are effectively enforced. Ensuring fairness, particularly in terms of access and opportunity, is key to fostering a digital environment that is equitable and inclusive.

Lastly, regulators should promote research into the societal impacts of emerging technologies. This not only informs policymaking but also helps anticipate and mitigate potential harms. Interdisciplinary research that brings together technologists, social scientists, ethicists, and legal scholars can provide valuable insights into the complex interplay between technology, society, and the law.

In the future, we may also see a move toward more anticipatory regulation – rather than reactive. This is particularly crucial given the rapid pace of technological evolution. Proactive regulatory strategies could involve ongoing risk assessments, scenario planning, and the early implementation of protective measures for technologies in their nascent stages. These tactics not only prevent harmful consequences but also build public trust in the deployment of new technologies.

In addition, digital literacy must be integrated as a core aspect of education. As users become more aware of their digital rights and responsibilities, they can make more informed decisions and hold tech companies accountable for any transgressions. Regulators should work closely with educators and tech companies to develop comprehensive digital literacy programs.

The issue of jurisdiction in the internet domain is also a significant challenge that needs to be addressed. The borderless nature of the internet often leaves gaps in the application and enforcement of laws. Legislations and treaties that address these jurisdictional issues, while respecting the sovereignty of nations and the global nature of the internet, will be a vital part of future internet regulation.

Another crucial proposal pertains to the issue of accessibility. Laws and regulations must ensure that digital platforms are accessible to all, regardless of physical abilities or linguistic skills. Regulatory frameworks must be put in place to ensure that all websites, online platforms, and digital services are designed and developed in a way that complies with universally accepted accessibility standards.

As we forge ahead into the future, a balanced and adaptive approach to internet regulation is essential. This approach requires a keen understanding of technological trends, a commitment to fundamental principles of justice and fairness, and an open, inclusive dialogue among all stakeholders. As we navigate this journey, we must bear in mind that the ultimate goal of internet regulation is not to stifle innovation, but to ensure that technology serves humanity in a way that respects our rights, protects our freedoms, and enhances our collective well-being.

As daunting as this task may seem, it presents a unique opportunity to redefine our societal norms and reshape our future. In the words of Tim Berners-Lee, the inventor of the World Wide Web, "The future is still so much bigger than the past." As we venture into this uncharted territory, we carry the responsibility and the power to ensure that our digital future is one that honors our shared values, safeguards our rights, and brings us closer together as a global community.

A New Era of Cybersecurity Challenges

As we step into the next chapter of the sentient web, a constellation of fresh cybersecurity challenges is emerging on the horizon. From the proliferation of interconnected devices to the advent of quantum computing, these novel facets of digital technology bring with them a host of security implications.

The first key challenge is the dramatic rise in the Internet of Things (IoT). This evolving landscape where everyday objects—ranging from home appliances to industrial machines—are connected to the internet, collecting, and exchanging data, opens up new frontiers for cybersecurity threats. Each connected device is a potential entry point for malicious actors, and securing these numerous devices becomes increasingly complex. Moreover, many IoT devices lack adequate security features, and their widespread adoption often outpaces the implementation of necessary safeguards.

Alongside the rise of IoT, advances in artificial intelligence and machine learning also present cybersecurity challenges. While AI can be a powerful tool in identifying and countering threats, its very same capabilities can be weaponized by malicious actors. Sophisticated AI systems can be used to automate attacks, craft persuasive phishing emails, or manipulate audio and video content to create deepfakes—hyper-realistic media forgeries that can deceive detection systems or individuals.

The development of quantum computing presents another significant challenge. Quantum computers have the potential to complete complex computations exponentially faster than current computers, which poses a serious threat to cryptographic systems. Current encryption methods that would take traditional computers millennia to crack could potentially be solved by quantum computers in seconds. Preparing our cybersecurity infrastructure for the era of quantum computing is, therefore, a daunting but essential task.

The cyber landscape is also being reshaped by shifts in geopolitical power and changes in the global economy. State-sponsored cyberattacks have become a prominent part of modern warfare and international relations. Governments worldwide are grappling with these incursions that blur the lines between warfare and diplomacy, and international law struggles to keep pace.

The increasingly digital economy, fueled by the rise of cryptocurrencies and non-fungible tokens (NFTs), introduces novel financial security concerns. The decentralization and anonymity of blockchain technology, while offering many advantages, also provide a platform for illicit activities, including money laundering, ransomware attacks, and financial fraud.

In addition to these emerging technological challenges, we are also dealing with a persistent cybersecurity skills gap. There is a shortage of cybersecurity professionals equipped to tackle these evolving threats. The rapid growth of technology and its infiltration into every aspect of our lives has outstripped our capacity to provide a skilled cybersecurity workforce.

Responding to these challenges requires a multi-faceted approach. It necessitates investment in cybersecurity education and training to fill the skills gap. A stronger emphasis on secure-by-design principles in the production of IoT devices is needed to ensure that security is an integral part of the design and development process rather than an afterthought.

Anticipatory regulation and international cooperation are essential to address state-sponsored cyberattacks and the security implications of a digital economy. Additionally, research into post-quantum cryptography—encryption that can withstand attacks from quantum computers—is vital.

Addressing these challenges is not solely the responsibility of tech companies, governments, or cybersecurity professionals. It also requires a digitally literate public aware of basic cybersecurity practices. After all, the weakest link in many security systems is not technological but human.

The new era of cybersecurity is characterized by its complexity and interconnectivity. The challenges are manifold, but they offer opportunities for innovation, collaboration, and growth. As we continue to navigate the digital revolution, the words of the ancient Greek playwright Sophocles echo as a reminder: "Look and you will find it - what is unsought will go undetected." Our collective task is to seek, detect, and protect against the cybersecurity threats of the new era, creating a safe and secure sentient web.

The digital realm is continuously evolving, and with it, cybersecurity challenges multiply and transform. Yet, these hurdles are not insurmountable. They are signals that call for increased vigilance, resourcefulness, and strategic planning. Like many other aspects of our lives, balancing technological advancement with security is a complex yet rewarding endeavor.

Among these challenges lies the crux of user empowerment. In the midst of these technological advancements and complex cybersecurity threats, it is crucial that users are not left feeling powerless or confused. Users need to be educated about these challenges and the steps they can take to protect themselves.

This could involve more sophisticated password practices, understanding the fundamentals of secure internet usage, or even knowing how to recognize and respond to phishing attempts.

Likewise, industry leaders and policymakers must ensure transparency in their operations. As users, the public has a right to know how their data is being secured and what measures are being taken to protect them from cyber threats. Transparency builds trust, and trust is essential in maintaining the resilience of the digital ecosystem in the face of cybersecurity threats.

Moreover, the public and private sectors should invest in research and development to stay ahead of cybercriminals. Innovative cybersecurity solutions, including artificial intelligence and machine learning applications, need to be explored and deployed not just to respond to the current threats, but also to anticipate future challenges.

Furthermore, collaboration is key. The interconnectedness that characterizes the digital world means that no single entity can single-handedly overcome these challenges. Governments, private sector organizations, academia, and individuals must work together. This collaboration could involve sharing knowledge, resources, or best practices.

Lastly, regulations must keep up with advancements in technology. Policymakers should ensure that there are comprehensive and up-to-date laws that deter cybercrime and protect users without stifling innovation. The development of these regulations should involve stakeholders from various sectors, including technology, law enforcement, academia, and civil society.

In the face of these evolving cybersecurity challenges, we are all at the frontline. From individual users to large corporations, from hackers in the shadows to policymakers in the spotlight, each one of us has a role to play.

Together, we can ensure that this new era of the sentient web is not only characterized by unprecedented technological advancement but also by an equally unprecedented level of cybersecurity.

In this digital era, the cybersecurity challenges we face are indeed considerable, but they also present opportunities. Opportunities for innovation, for collaboration, for education, and for the establishment of new norms.

By facing these challenges head-on, we can ensure that the sentient web, and our future within it, is marked not by insecurity and uncertainty, but by trust, resilience, and an empowered digital citizenry.

Chapter 7: The Future of the Sentient Web

Technological Advancements and Their Implications for the Sentient Web

As we delve into the future of the sentient web, we must recognize that our digital universe is influenced, and in turn shapes, a plethora of interconnected factors - societal, economic, technological, political, and ethical. The technological advancements heralding the sentient web era pose significant questions concerning agency, autonomy, and identity that we, as a global community, need to address together.

The concept of a sentient web might sound like the premise for a science fiction novel, but it's becoming more tangible as technology advances at an unprecedented pace. Driven by AI, machine learning, and data analytics, the sentient web is envisioned as an interconnected digital environment that can perceive, interact, learn, and adapt.

AI, Machine Learning, and Data Analytics

AI, machine learning, and data analytics are the primary drivers of this sentient web. Their advances not only contribute to the evolving digital landscape but also underline the intricate challenges and opportunities that lay ahead.

AI has come a long way from its inception. Today's AI can understand, learn, predict, and potentially function independently. Its ability to learn and adapt has been facilitated by another significant trend, machine learning. Machine learning algorithms use data to improve their performance over time without being explicitly programmed to do so. These systems learn from experience and refine their insights and predictions each time they're fed new data.

The convergence of AI and machine learning with data analytics has led to the rise of more sophisticated, predictive, and personalized digital experiences. These advancements underpin a key component of the sentient web – its ability to understand and respond to users' needs in an autonomous, adaptive, and possibly proactive manner.

Internet of Things (IoT) and 5G

The proliferation of IoT devices and the advent of 5G are critical factors shaping the sentient web's landscape. IoT devices – from smart home appliances to industrial sensors – provide the data necessary for the sentient web's 'understanding' and 'learning'. The more devices we have in the digital ecosystem, the more data the sentient web can analyze and learn from.

5G, with its high speed and low latency, allows these devices to communicate and share data in real-time, a vital aspect of a sentient web that can respond and adapt instantaneously. The synergy between IoT and 5G can turn the concept of the sentient web from an abstract idea into a palpable reality.

Blockchain and Distributed Ledger Technology (DLT)

The integration of blockchain and DLT in the sentient web framework introduces a new level of transparency, accountability, and security. Blockchain's decentralized nature can mitigate some of the challenges posed by a centralized data processing system, such as single points of failure or control.

Quantum Computing

Quantum computing, still in its early stages, has the potential to exponentially increase computational power, opening up new possibilities for the sentient web. This would vastly speed up data processing and complex calculations that underpin AI and machine learning, potentially enabling the sentient web to 'think' and 'learn' even more quickly and efficiently.

As we move forward, we must grapple with these technological advancements' implications. They promise improved efficiency, convenience, and personalization but also introduce new ethical and practical challenges. As we embrace this sentient web era, we need to carefully navigate the delicate balance between technological progress and its implications on our society, economy, and personal lives.

In the end, the sentient web's future should not be a dystopian landscape of machines ruling humans, but rather a harmonious co-existence where technology enhances human capabilities and enriches our lives. For this to happen, we need an open, ongoing conversation involving technologists, ethicists, policymakers, businesses, and the general public. This collective intelligence will be our guiding compass as we navigate the complex ethical and practical implications of the sentient web.

Cybersecurity and Data Privacy

The sentient web's dependence on data raises significant cybersecurity and data privacy concerns. These technologies will have access to enormous amounts of personal, sensitive, and potentially intrusive data. With an increase in data traffic, the chances of data breaches, cyber-attacks, and misuse of personal information also rise. Ensuring that robust cybersecurity measures and privacy-enhancing technologies are integral to the sentient web design will be paramount.

Human Agency and Autonomy

As the sentient web learns and adapts, it will potentially have the ability to make predictions and even decisions on behalf of users. This raises critical questions about human agency and autonomy. How much control are we willing to relinquish to intelligent machines? What decisions should we reserve for humans, and which can we safely delegate to AI? These questions require careful deliberation, balancing the benefits of automation and efficiency against the importance of preserving human agency.

Ethics and Accountability

The sentient web's ability to 'learn' and 'make decisions' brings forth ethical considerations and questions about accountability. If an AI-based decision leads to negative outcomes, who is accountable - the AI, the developers, the users? Establishing ethical guidelines and accountability mechanisms will be critical in the sentient web era.

Digital Divide and Inequality

Lastly, we must consider the potential of these advancements to exacerbate digital divides and inequalities. The benefits of the sentient web could disproportionately go to those with access to the latest technologies, leaving behind those who are digitally disadvantaged. Ensuring equitable access to the benefits of the sentient web must be a core priority.

As we journey towards the future of the sentient web, these considerations guide us. We must keep them in mind while designing and implementing these advanced technologies, thereby shaping a future where technology serves humanity and not the other way around.

The future of the sentient web is laden with possibilities that can redefine our interaction with the digital realm. As we move towards this exciting future, we must not lose sight of the interconnected web of ethical and practical considerations that this journey entails. Let us move forward with an open mind, an eagerness to learn, and a commitment to create a sentient web that is a force for good, ensuring a harmonious coexistence of humanity and technology. It's not just about navigating the challenges; it's about shaping the opportunities to build a future we all want to be part of.

Ethical Considerations for Future Internet Development

As we consider the future of the internet and our evolving digital landscape, it becomes evident that our technological capabilities are outpacing the ethical frameworks that guide them. The lightning-fast development of new technologies, coupled with the increasing integration of artificial intelligence into our daily lives, necessitates a deep and thoughtful examination of the ethical implications of this progress.

In the early stages of the internet, the primary concerns were around access and functionality. Fast-forward a few decades, and our focus has expanded to issues of privacy, data security, misinformation, algorithmic bias, and the digital divide. These concerns underscore the need for a robust ethical framework to guide the future development of the internet.

Data Privacy and Security

At the core of future internet development is data – our digital footprints. Every click, like, share, and comment contributes to the vast, uncharted universe of data. Data is what fuels the predictive powers of AI and machine learning algorithms. It personalizes our digital experiences, making them more seamless and efficient. However, this tremendous power comes with considerable responsibility. How do we protect this data from misuse? How do we balance the benefits of personalization with the inherent right to privacy?

The answer lies in establishing strong data governance structures that prioritize privacy and consent. Companies must be transparent about the data they collect and how they use it. Further, they must obtain informed consent from users, providing them with meaningful control over their data. The 'privacy by design' principle, where privacy safeguards are incorporated into products from the get-go, needs to be the norm rather than the exception.

Algorithmic Fairness and Accountability

Algorithmic bias has emerged as a significant ethical concern in AI applications. If the data used to train AI models contains bias, the resulting algorithms will reflect and perpetuate these biases, leading to discriminatory outcomes. For instance, an AI model trained on data reflecting societal biases against a particular group may inadvertently deny them opportunities, whether it's job prospects, loans, or healthcare.

Addressing this issue requires a commitment to algorithmic fairness. AI developers must prioritize the elimination of bias in AI training data and algorithms. Further, there should be transparency about how algorithms make decisions and a mechanism for redress when algorithms produce unfair or harmful outcomes. Creating AI systems that are explainable, transparent, and accountable should be a key ethical consideration for future internet development.

Digital Equity

The digital divide refers to the gap between those who have access to the internet and digital technologies and those who do not. This divide often mirrors and exacerbates existing social, economic, and geographical inequalities. As the internet increasingly becomes the backbone of essential services like education, healthcare, and employment, the digital divide turns into a chasm of opportunity.

Future internet development must prioritize digital equity – ensuring that everyone, regardless of their location, economic status, or social circumstances, has access to the benefits of the internet. This includes affordable internet access, digital literacy programs, and inclusive design that takes into account the needs of all users, including those with disabilities.

Misinformation and Trust

The internet has democratized information access. However, it has also become a hotbed for misinformation and fake news. The rapid spread of false information can have dire consequences, from fueling social unrest to undermining public health efforts.

An ethical approach to future internet development must consider mechanisms to curb the spread of misinformation while respecting the principles of free speech and openness that the internet was built on. This could include better algorithms to detect and flag fake news, transparency about the sources of information, and digital literacy education to help users critically evaluate online content.

The ethical considerations for future internet development are vast and complex. They require the collaboration of all stakeholders – from technology developers to policymakers, educators, and consumers. A multi-stakeholder, inclusive approach can ensure that we harness the power of the internet while keeping in mind the principles of fairness, transparency, accountability, and respect for individual rights.

Future internet development cannot merely be about technological advancements. It needs to be human-centric, focusing on how technology can serve humanity rather than the other way around. Ethical considerations should be at the heart of technological innovation, not an afterthought. These principles should guide the development of laws, regulations, and guidelines that govern our digital future.

The aim should be to create a future internet that upholds and respects human rights, values, and dignity, a digital space where technology serves as a tool for empowerment rather than a means of exploitation. In this way, we can ensure that the future internet continues to be a force for good, contributing to human development and progress.

With these ethical considerations in mind, we can work towards a vision of the internet that truly embodies its founding ideals – a global, open, and inclusive platform that not only connects us but also respects our rights and freedoms. This is the future of the internet that we should aspire to, and it's up to us to make it a reality.

The Balancing Act: Human and Machine Agency in the Future Internet

As we embark on this journey into the era of a sentient web, the balance between human and machine agency presents a critical concern. There is an intricate dance in progress as we teeter between immense technological advancements and the preservation of fundamental human qualities. This act of balance is not a zero-sum game, where the rise of machines translates to the fall of humans.

Instead, it requires the reconciliation of the strength of machines and the uniqueness of human capabilities.

Consider the fundamental shift in the very nature of the internet. What started as a passive tool for information retrieval and communication has transformed into an active entity that learns, evolves, and makes decisions. Machine learning algorithms now curate our digital experiences, artificial intelligence aids in our decision-making processes, and autonomous systems carry out tasks with little to no human intervention.

The role of AI, machine learning, and the broader umbrella of autonomous systems within this sentient web comes with an essential realization: the inherent value of these systems lies in their ability to process, analyze and respond to vast quantities of data at speeds and scales that far outstrip human capability. This processing power extends from the trivial, such as suggesting the next song to play, to life-altering decisions such as diagnosing a critical illness or driving an autonomous vehicle.

However, the increasing reliance on AI systems raises essential questions about agency – who gets to make decisions, on what basis, and with what repercussions? The question becomes more complex when we factor in the nature of these AI systems – their decisions are not just based on pre-programmed responses but are a product of learning from vast data sets. This introduces a certain level of opacity and unpredictability, as these systems can evolve and adapt in ways that might not be entirely understandable, even to their creators.

In this context, balancing human and machine agency becomes an intricate task. On one hand, we have the tremendous potential of AI and autonomous systems to transform our lives in profound ways. They can make our lives more comfortable, our societies more efficient, and open up possibilities we have yet to imagine. On the other hand, the unchecked rise of machine agency could lead to significant challenges such as job displacement, privacy concerns, and potentially a loss of human agency.

So how do we balance these two opposing forces? The solution might lie in the principle of human-in-the-loop AI. This approach to AI development emphasizes that no matter how advanced these systems become, there should always be a role for human oversight, control, and decision-making. This means designing AI systems that are not just autonomous but also transparent, explainable, and accountable.

In the context of the sentient web, the human-in-the-loop approach can manifest in several ways. For instance, content moderation algorithms can make preliminary decisions based on their training, but human reviewers should be able to intervene, review, and correct these decisions. Similarly, autonomous vehicles should have mechanisms for human intervention in critical situations, or at the very least, provide clear and understandable information to the passengers about their decision-making processes.

The goal is not to curb the evolution or capabilities of AI and autonomous systems. Instead, it is about ensuring these systems serve our needs, respect our values, and preserve our agency. Technology should be a tool that humans use, not a master we serve.

As we ponder the future of the sentient web, this balance between human and machine agency will likely define our journey. We have the opportunity to create a future where technology amplifies human capabilities rather than replacing them, a future where the sentient web is a testament to human innovation and ingenuity, not a threat to our agency.

To achieve this future, we must remember that technology is not an end in itself, but a means to an end – the enrichment and betterment of the human experience. We must seek to forge a partnership between humans and machines, where each can leverage their unique strengths to create a balanced, symbiotic relationship. Humans bring to the table creativity, empathy, and subjective judgement, while machines provide computational power, speed, and the capacity to handle vast complexity.

However, ensuring this balance is not just a technological challenge, it is a socio-political one as well. It requires inclusive, democratic decision-making processes that involve all stakeholders – from policymakers and technologists to ordinary citizens. Only through such collective deliberation can we make decisions that reflect our shared values and aspirations for the sentient web.

In addition, as we forge this new human-machine partnership, we must ensure that the benefits are broadly distributed and accessible to all, not just a privileged few. This includes addressing the digital divide, ensuring access to technology, and creating opportunities for meaningful engagement with these systems. We must also guard against the abuse of these technologies, from invasion of privacy to the spread of misinformation. This calls for robust legal frameworks and regulatory mechanisms that can keep pace with the rapid advancement of technology.

Finally, we must invest in education and capacity building, so that everyone can understand, interact with, and shape these technological systems. This includes digital literacy programs, technology education, and creating spaces for public dialogue and deliberation about the role of technology in our lives.

The sentient web promises a future of incredible possibilities. But to navigate this future, we need to balance the immense potential of these technologies with the preservation of human agency. Only then can we ensure a future internet that is not just smart, but also wise; not just powerful, but also empowering. A future where technology serves us, not the other way around. The journey to this future is fraught with challenges, but it is a journey worth embarking upon. For at stake is not just the future of the internet, but the future of our societies, our values, and our shared humanity.

Final Thoughts: The Ongoing Journey of the Sentient Web

In concluding this exploration of the sentient web, its ethical implications, the interplay between human and machine agency, and the profound transformation it heralds, it's essential to pause and reflect. We stand at the precipice of a new era—an era that is as promising as it is challenging. The journey of the sentient web is an ongoing one, and we are collectively the navigators of its course.

The sentient web represents a profound shift in our understanding of technology's role in our lives. It's no longer merely a tool we use, but an environment we inhabit, a partner we collaborate with, and a reflection of our collective desires and fears. This paradigm shift calls for a similarly profound shift in our attitudes, policies, and behaviors. It requires us to renegotiate our relationship with technology, to ensure it serves us, and not the other way around.

The transformative power of the sentient web lies in its potential to democratize knowledge and empower individuals. However, its very ubiquity and sophistication make it ripe for exploitation and misuse. To navigate this dichotomy, we need to develop robust ethical and regulatory frameworks that are as dynamic, inclusive, and forward-thinking as the technology itself. This demands a concerted, collective effort from all stakeholders – policymakers, technologists, businesses, and civil society.

In a world increasingly mediated by intelligent machines, preserving human agency becomes paramount. We must strive for a balance where technology augments human capabilities without eroding human autonomy. This involves making difficult choices about the trade-offs between convenience and control, between personalization and privacy, between openness and security. But these are choices we must make, for at stake is not just the future of the internet, but the kind of society we want to live in.

The digital divide is another key challenge. As the web becomes more sentient, there's a risk that those without access to technology, or the skills to use it, could be left behind. Bridging this divide calls for substantial investments in infrastructure, education, and capacity building. It also calls for innovative solutions that make technology accessible and user-friendly for all.

The sentient web also raises intriguing questions about identity, personhood, and rights in the digital age. As we interact with increasingly sophisticated AI, we will need to redefine these concepts to account for new realities. This includes grappling with issues like data ownership, algorithmic accountability, digital rights, and the ethics of AI.

Perhaps the most profound challenge of the sentient web is the pace of change itself. Technology is evolving at breakneck speed, often outpacing our ability to understand its implications, let alone regulate it effectively. Keeping pace with this change requires not just technological savvy, but also wisdom, foresight, and a deep understanding of human values.

In the face of these challenges, it's easy to feel overwhelmed. But we should also feel inspired. For the sentient web offers us an unprecedented opportunity to shape our destiny, to reimagine our societies, and to create a future that reflects our highest ideals. The sentient web is not just a technological phenomenon, it's a human endeavor. Its future will be shaped by the choices we make, the values we uphold, and the visions we aspire to.

In closing, the journey of the sentient web is indeed a journey into the unknown. But it's also a journey towards a horizon filled with promise. It is an ongoing journey that will continue to evolve and surprise us, challenging us to adapt, learn, and grow. As we embark on this journey, let's do so with curiosity, courage, and a commitment to making the sentient web a force for good. Let us strive to create a future where technology is not just smart, but also wise; not just powerful, but also empowering. A future that honors and amplifies our shared humanity, rather than diluting or overshadowing it.

As we ponder the myriad possibilities the sentient web offers, it's essential to remain centered on human values.

Technology is a reflection of our collective aspirations, a mirror to our intentions, and a tool for our creative expression. As we guide its evolution, let us ensure that it remains rooted in principles of fairness, justice, respect, and mutual understanding.

Looking forward, there's much to do. Ensuring effective regulation, fostering inclusivity, promoting digital literacy, and safeguarding digital rights—these tasks fall upon all of us. We must collectively rise to the occasion, harnessing our strengths and insights to navigate the complexities and uncertainties of this new digital landscape. Governments, businesses, academics, civil society, and individuals—all have crucial roles to play in this grand endeavor.

In all of this, the role of education cannot be overemphasized. As the sentient web evolves, so must our understanding of it. We need to equip current and future generations with the necessary skills and knowledge to navigate the sentient web responsibly and effectively. This includes not only technical skills, but also a deep understanding of digital ethics, data privacy, and cyber hygiene.

The security of the sentient web also deserves special attention. As our dependence on the web deepens, so does our vulnerability to cyber threats. Robust cybersecurity measures are essential to protect individuals, institutions, and infrastructure from these threats. But equally important is fostering a culture of security, where all users understand their responsibilities in maintaining the integrity and safety of the digital ecosystem.

We must also stay vigilant against the erosion of privacy in the digital age. With personal data increasingly becoming a currency of the web, we must champion policies and practices that respect and protect individuals' rights to their data. This includes advocating for more transparent and ethical data handling practices, and empowering individuals to take control of their digital identities.

The sentient web is a testament to human ingenuity and a beacon of human potential. Its journey is our journey. As we continue to explore its depths, let us strive to make it a platform for positive transformation, a tool for enlightenment, and a catalyst for a more just, equitable, and sustainable future.

Finally, as we ponder the journey of the sentient web, we must remember that the destination is not as important as the journey itself. The sentient web is a process, an evolution, a continuous interplay between humans and technology. The choices we make, the principles we uphold, the values we champion—these will define the path we traverse and the milestones we reach.

In closing, let us remember that the sentient web is not just about technology—it's about us. It's about our ability to imagine, innovate, and inspire. It's about our capacity for empathy, compassion, and connection. It's about our commitment to justice, equality, and dignity. As we forge ahead on this exciting journey, let us strive to create a sentient web that reflects the best of who we are, and the world we wish to live in.

The journey of the sentient web is a testament to the power of human imagination, the resilience of human spirit, and the boundless potential of human ingenuity.

As we continue on this path, let us carry with us a sense of hope, a spirit of collaboration, and a commitment to building a future that truly benefits all of humanity.

For the sentient web is not just a product of our technological prowess, but a reflection of our shared dreams, our common aspirations, and our collective will to create a world that is more connected, more enlightened, and more humane.

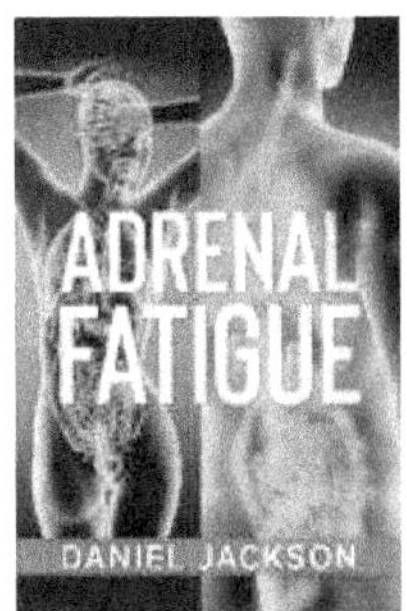

Take a look at more great books available from Rockwood Publishing

... **some for FREE!**

Just visit the link below:

rockwoodpublishing.co.uk

has been compiled to give an overview of the subject(s) and detail some of the symptoms, treatments etc. that are available to people with this condition. It is not intended to give medical advice. For a firm diagnosis of your condition, and for a treatment plan suitable for you, you should consult your doctor or consultant. The writer of this book and the publisher are not responsible for any damages or negative consequences following any of the treatments or methods highlighted in this book. Website links are for informational purposes and should not be seen as a personal endorsement; the same applies to the products detailed in this book. The reader should also be aware that although the web links included were correct at the time of writing, they may become out of date in the future.

Disclaimers

The content contained within this book is for information and entertainment purposes only, and in no way purports to represent professional medical opinion. It should NOT be used as a substitute for expert advice, and you must consult with your designated health professional before acting upon any information contained herein or before undertaking any practice whose methodology is referred to in this book. The author is NOT a registered health professional and the text merely represents personal opinion, not medical fact. The author cannot be held responsible for the consequences of any action derived from the reading of this book, as the content is not based on diagnosis and subsequent regimen. It is the reader's responsibility to seek proper, professional medical advice from a registered health practitioner in connection with any material contained within this book.

Legal Disclaimer (part 1)

Nothing in this book should be construed as an attempt to diagnose, treat or cure. The information in this book is intended to be a community resource. The author takes no responsibility for any informational material or brochures produced using information taken from this book. The author has endeavoured to ensure that all information is correct at the time of publication. This information, however, is subject to change without notice. The author makes no warranty with regard to the accuracy of any information and will not be liable for any errors or omissions. Any liability that arises as a result of this information is hereby excluded to the fullest extent allowed by law.

This information should not be used as a substitute for seeking independent professional advice.

Legal Disclaimer (part 2)

Disclaimer and Terms of Use:

a) i. In publishing this information, the author makes no representations concerning the efficacy, appropriateness or suitability of any products or treatments. Use this information at your own risk. The compiler is not a doctor and has no medical background or training.

ii. Statements and information regarding dietary supplements, books and any products mentioned have not been evaluated by any health authority and are not intended to diagnose, treat, cure or prevent any disease or health condition.

b) In view of the possibility of human error, neither the author nor any other party involved in providing this information, warrant that the information contained therein is in every respect accurate or complete and they are not responsible nor liable for any errors or omissions that may be found or for the results obtained from the use of such information. The entire risk as to use of this information is assumed by the user.

c) You are encouraged to consult other sources and confirm the information.

d) The information you access is provided "as is". No warranty, expressed or implied, is given as to the accuracy, completeness or timeliness of any information herein, or for obtaining legal advice. To the fullest extent permissible pursuant to applicable law, neither the author nor any other parties who have been involved in the creation, preparation, printing, or delivering of this information assume responsibility for the completeness, accuracy, timeliness, errors or omissions of said information and assume no liability for any direct, incidental, consequential, indirect, or punitive damages as well as any circumstance for any complication, injuries, side effects or other medical accidents to person or property arising from or in connection with the use or reliance upon any information contained herein.

e) The author is not responsible for the contents of any linked site or any link contained in a linked site, or any changes or update to such sites. The inclusion of any link does not imply endorsement by the author. The author makes no representations or claims as to the quality, content and accuracy of the information, services, products, messages which may be provided by such resources, and specifically disclaims any warranties, including but not limited to implied or express warranties of merchantability or fitness for any particular usage, application or purpose.

f) The information provided is general in nature and is intended for educational and informational purposes only. It is not intended to replace or substitute the evaluation, judgment, diagnosis, and medical or preventative care of a physician, paediatrician, therapist and/or health care provider.

g) Any medical, nutritional, dietetic, therapeutic or other decisions, dosages, treatments or drug regimes should be made in consultation with a health care practitioner. Do not discontinue treatment or medication without first consulting your physician, clinician or therapist.

h) By reading this information, you signify your assent to these terms and conditions of use. If you do not agree to these terms and conditions of use, do not read/use this information. If any provision of these terms and conditions of use shall be determined to be unlawful, void or for any reason unenforceable, then that provision shall be deemed severable from this agreement and shall not affect the validity and enforceability of any remaining provisions.

i) The information, services, products, messages and other materials, individually and collectively, are provided with the understanding that the author is not engaged in rendering medical advice or recommendations.

j) The information and the terms of use are subject to change without notice. The material provided as is without warranty of any kind and may include inaccuracies and/or typographical errors. The author makes no representations about the suitability of this information for any purpose. The author disclaims all warranties with regard to this information, including all implied warranties, and in no event shall the author be held liable, resulting from, or in any way related to, the use of this information.

k) The unauthorized alteration of the content of this information is expressly prohibited. The author, its agents and representatives shall not be responsible for any claims, actions or damages which may arise on account of the unauthorized alteration of this information.

www.ingramcontent.com/pod-product-compliance
Lightning Source LLC
Chambersburg PA
CBHW071425150726
48000CB00001B/478